PAPIER-MACHE
PROJECT BOOK

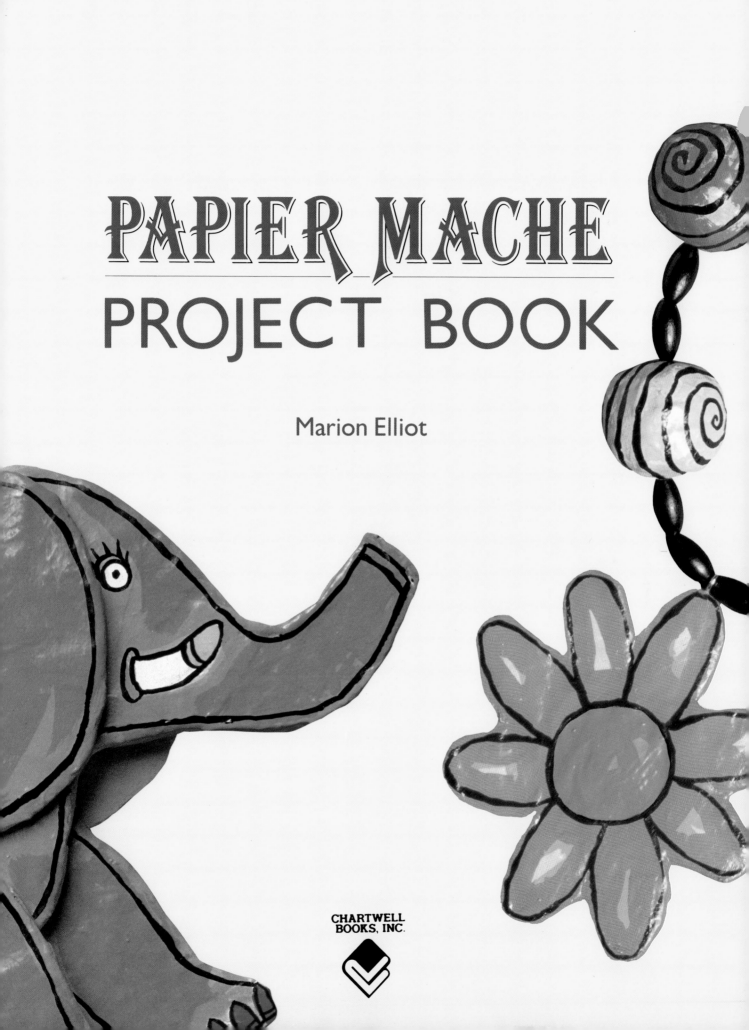

PAPIER MACHE
PROJECT BOOK

Marion Elliot

CHARTWELL
BOOKS, INC.

A QUINTET BOOK

Published by Chartwell Books
A Division of Book Sales, Inc.
110 Enterprise Avenue
Secaucus, New Jersey 07094

This edition produced for sale in the U.S.A., its
territories and dependencies only.

ISBN–1–55521–773–7

This book was designed and produced by
Quintet Publishing Limited
6 Blundell Street
London N7 9BH

Creative Director: Richard Dewing
Designer: James Lawrence
Project Editor: Stefanie Foster
Editor: Lydia Darbyshire
Photographer: Ian Howes

Typeset in Great Britain by
Central Southern Typesetters, Eastbourne
Manufactured in Hong Kong by
Regent Publishing Services Limited
Printed in Hong Kong by
Leefung-Asco Printers Limited

CONTENTS

What is Papier Mâché? 6

Getting Started
Materials 8
Techniques 11

Plate and Bowl 14

Plate 15
Barnacle Bowl 18

Jewellery 22

Earrings 23
Bangles 26
Necklace 30
Brooch 34

Boxes 37

Jewelled Box 38
Pen and Pencil Tray 41
Hinged Box 45
Heart-shaped Box 48

Frames 52

Heart-shaped Frame 53
Square Frame with
    Heart-shaped Opening 58

Festivals 61

Christmas Cut-outs 62
Easter Eggs 65
Easter Bunny 69

Toys 73

Articulated Elephant 74
Face Mask 78
Monster Mask 82
Mobile 85
Puppets 90

WHAT IS PAPIER-MACHE?

E very year, millions of tons of waste paper are thrown away – here are lots of fun and creative ways of recycling some of it!

Papier-mâché, which is French for "chewed paper," is an exciting way to make something new out of waste paper, and there are two main methods of making it – pulping and layering.

For the pulping method, small pieces of paper are soaked in water until they disintegrate. Then they are mashed into a pulp, drained, squeezed almost dry, and mixed with glue. Watered-down white craft glue is most suitable for this purpose. The resulting pulp can be pressed into greased molds or used to add details to objects made by the layering method. If small amounts of pulp are needed, you can take a pasted strip of paper and scrunch it between your fingers to form a pellet of pulp.

The second method, layering, is the main method used in this book for making papier-mâché. This involves

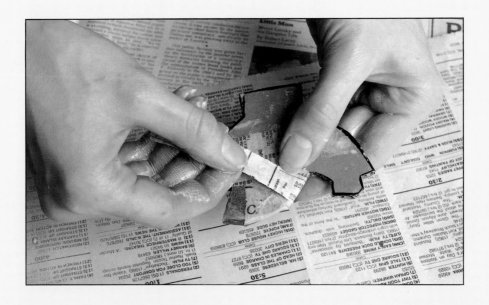

sticking strips of torn paper together and results in a very tough, but light, substance. Sometimes pulp is used to add details to some of the projects.

There are more than 20 projects for you to try, but these are only the beginning. You'll have plenty of your own ideas once you start work, and as your confidence grows and you become more competent, you'll probably be keen to experiment with your new skills. You might even like to adapt the projects to reflect your own hobbies and interests.

The first two sections describe all the materials and techniques you will need to make papier-mâché. These are followed by the projects themselves, with ideas for special events and occasions, toys to make, jewelry to wear, boxes and frames of various kinds, and, to start you off, a simple plate and a bowl.

It is a good idea to read the techniques section thoroughly before you embark on any projects so that you become familiar with the basic skills required and the materials you will need. Even if things seem a little messy at first, it is worth persevering – you will find that it is great fun making your own creations from papier-mâché!

GETTING STARTED

What you need

Paper

First, and most obviously, you will need paper! All sorts of paper are suitable, and different papers will give different results. Collect a variety of papers – newspaper, computer printout paper, brown wrapping paper and even telephone directories – and test them for suitability. The lighter and thinner the paper you use, the smoother your finished objects will be.

For layering, where strips of paper are pasted on top of each other, it is best to use newspaper, as the layers bond together well and stick smoothly. Nearly everyone reads newspapers, so you shouldn't have any trouble collecting some! For pulping, where small pieces of paper are soaked in water, squeezed almost dry and mixed with glue, you can use almost any kind of paper, but do avoid all paper that is waxed or has a waterproof finish – this will look shiny – as it is not possible to break it down by soaking in water. As a general rule, the smoother and whiter the paper you use, the finer the pulp will be. Experiment with a variety of papers to discover which effects you like best.

Glue

So, having collected all your paper, you will need glue to stick it together. The best choice is cold-water wallpaper paste – be careful to use a brand that is nontoxic though. Wallpaper paste is easy to mix, and leftovers can be stored in an airtight container. If you spill some on your clothes, it won't stain, and it washes out easily. An alternative to wallpaper paste is sticky white craft glue. If you use it for making papier-mâché, you will need to dilute it first, by adding about twice as much water as glue. This glue dries more quickly than wallpaper paste and results in stronger papier-mâché, but it does have one big disadvantage: splashes won't wash out of clothes, carpets, or upholstery once they have dried, and you could become highly unpopular if you accidentally spill some! Again, if you do use white glue, remember to choose a nontoxic brand.

Apart from undiluted white glue, which is used in some projects to stick pieces of cardboard together, several projects also need nontoxic, strong, clear adhesive. Several brands of clear glue are suitable, but never use an epoxy-resin glue.

HELPFUL HINT . . .

If possible, use different colored paper for each layer of papier-mâché – it will enable you to see if you've completely covered the object with one layer before you begin the next and help to prevent uneven patches.

Equipment

Now that you have your main ingredients, you will also need some basic equipment. You will probably already have some **rulers** and **pencils**. Plastic rulers are fine for measuring pieces of cardboard, transferring measurements and so on, but when you have to cut straight lines, you should use a metal ruler. Your plastic ruler will eventually become chipped if you cut against it with a craft knife.

To mix the glue, whether you are using wallpaper paste or white glue, you will need a **large plastic bowl**. A sink bowl is perfect, although it is a good idea to keep it to one side reserved especially for glue and to avoid using it for washing the dishes in, too.

A **craft knife** is very useful for cutting cardboard, especially if you are using the heavy-duty kind. However, you must be very, very careful with these knives, as their blades are extremely sharp. Always get an adult to help you at this stage in a project to prevent accidents.

You will need some **petroleum jelly** to grease molds before you put papier-mâché into them. The jelly creates a barrier between the mold and the paper, allowing the paper shape to be removed easily when it is dry – rather like a cake from a cake pan.

Modeling clay is very useful for making large, three-dimensional items such as puppet heads. You can make a sort of mold for the head by modeling it in clay first and then covering it with several layers of papier-mâché. Allow the paper to dry thoroughly, and then cut it open and remove the clay. Join the paper halves back together with strips of pasted paper. You can add facial features – ears and a nose, for example – to the head with small pellets of paper pulp.

A **palette-knife** with a thin blade is useful for helping to remove dry papier-mâché shapes from the sides of molds and for prising clay from the inside of finished pieces.

A **wire cake rack** is ideal for drying smaller items because it allows air to circulate freely around them. The pieces can be removed quite easily when they are dry.

Scissors are handy for cutting around shapes made from thin cardboard. Don't, however, use scissors to cut paper into strips – it should always be torn.

The finished projects are decorated with **poster paint**. There is a wide choice of colors available, but remember to check that you are using a nontoxic brand. The same applies to the **black India ink** that is used to outline designs – always use a nontoxic brand.

Masking tape is used in many of the projects to hold sections of cardboard together while they are drying. You can peel the tape from the card once the glue has set, but it will give extra strength to your constructions if you leave it in place and simply paper over it.

Cardboard is used to make the basic structure in several projects. Two different weights are used: **heavy corrugated cardboard** for larger items like the puppet theater, where strength is needed to avoid warping, and **thinner card** for such projects as the Christmas decorations, earrings, and brooch. Empty boxes from the supermarket, electrical goods stores, and the like are ideal for heavy cardboard as long as they are clean and uncreased.

Clear gloss varnish was used to seal most of the projects in this book and to give them an attractive, shiny surface. Use a nontoxic brand. It is possible to buy a type of varnish that is made specifically for paper crafts such as papier-mâché, and this is quite safe. As with all the paints, glues, and inks used for these projects, an educational supplier or art store with a children's section will be able to tell you which brands are suitable. However, if you use a varnish that can only be cleaned off brushes with turpentine, ask an adult to help you, as turpentine can be dangerous if it is handled carelessly.

HELPFUL HINT . . .

Always use nontoxic glues and paints. Ask the store clerk for advice if you're in any doubt.

Techniques

Before you start any of the projects, read through all the instructions carefully to check how long the project will take you – many stages need to dry out overnight, so it is best to plan ahead.

Tearing paper

The length and width of your paper strips will vary according to what you are making. Pieces up to 3 in. (7.5cm) wide can be used if you are covering large, flat surfaces, but you will often find that you need much smaller pieces, some only as large as postage stamps.

When you are tearing up paper, bear in mind that it has a grain, like fabric, and it will tear much more easily in one direction than the other, usually – though not always – from the top to the bottom. Never cut paper into strips with scissors; this will give it a blunt, hard edge, which will show up when your object is painted and varnished.

Tear along the correct grain of the paper, as in the top picture. You can see, in the bottom picture, what happens if you do it the wrong way!

HELPFUL HINT . . .

Wash your hands when you have been tearing up newspaper. You will be surprised at how much ink comes off the paper!

Gluing

Your strips of paper should be covered on both sides with wallpaper paste or watered-down white glue. You can use your fingers or a brush to apply the glue, but don't use too much, or your object will take a long time to dry.

HELPFUL HINT . . .

Cover your worktop or table with old newspaper to prevent it from getting marked with splashes of glue or paint. Best of all, use a plastic sheet, which can be wiped clean when you have finished work for the day.

Using a mold

All sorts of objects can be used as molds for papier-mâché. Bowls, plates, and dishes are ideal. Always smear petroleum jelly over the mold before you use it, or it will be very difficult to remove the dried paper shape. Cardboard is also a good "mold" or base – but it will be left inside the paper as a permanent part of the structure. Several layers can be built up on top of cardboard to make a good, strong base.

Drying

The time each piece will take to dry will depend on its size and the number of layers of papier-mâché you have used. Usually, 24 hours is adequate for a cardboard shape with two or three layers of paper on it, but a balloon with eight layers of papier-mâché may take up to 3 days to dry. Use a warm place to dry your papier-mâché.

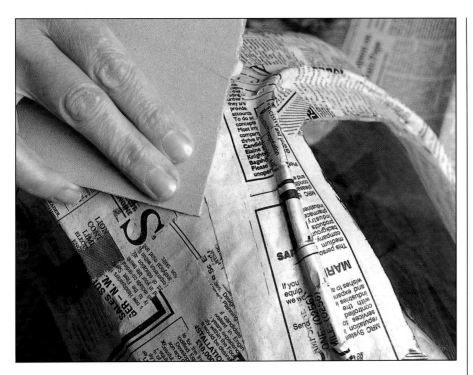

HELPFUL HINT . . .

Wear a plastic apron or a pair of overalls when you make papier-mâché – it can be quite messy.

Sanding

When your papier-mâché is dry, you should lightly rub down the surface with fine sandpaper. This will remove any wrinkles in the paper and give you a smoother surface to paint on.

Priming

Use two coats of white paint to prime the surface of your papier-mâché. This will cover up newsprint effectively, gives a bright ground to paint on, and will make your colors seem more luminous. You must let the first coat dry before adding the second, or the paint may crack. If this happens, let the paint dry, sand it back to the paper, and start again. Always use nontoxic paint.

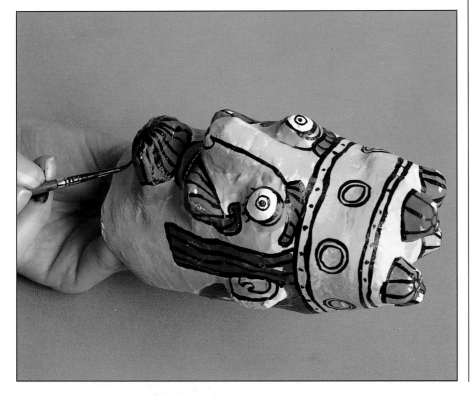

Decorating

When you have primed the papier-mâché, it can be decorated with poster paint. You will have to thin the paint with water, and you will probably need to use two coats to achieve a good, deep color. Black India ink, which is waterproof, can be used to accentuate the painted designs. Apply it with a thin paint-brush and use a nontoxic brand.

PLATE & BOWL

These two projects will introduce you to the basic techniques you will be using to make papier-mâché. The first, a plate, involves very simple layering into a greased mold, while the second, a bowl, requires the use of two molds.

The plate shape is left quite plain, and when its edges have been sealed with paper strips to stop it from "unraveling," it is decorated and varnished. The outside of the bowl is decorated with small lumps of papier-mâché, and the rim, middle and base, are trimmed with cord to make it looks sturdier.

The molds are simple household items – bowls and dishes – that you might find in the kitchen. They are very plain, but spend a little time and thought to discover combinations of molds that will look good together and produce interesting and original results.

You could even use molds in the shape of fish and animals, or items like heart-shaped cake pans, but be sure to ask permission before you start work or you may be banned from the kitchen!

Plate

This is a very simple project to teach you the basics of papier-mâché, and it involves the process known as layering, by which strips of paper are laid on top of one another to form a strong paper shell.

The plate is decorated in bold, cheerful colors, and it is sealed with two coats of clear gloss varnish. Although you should not put wet things on it, the plate would hold fruit or something similar, or it could be hung on a wall as a decorative plaque. You could make several, painting them to match the color scheme of a bedroom or the kitchen.

Making the plate

1 Grease the plate you are using as your mold with a thin layer of petroleum jelly. This will make it easy to release the finished plate shape from the mold when it has dried. Tear the paper into strips about 1 in. (2.5cm) wide and long enough to stretch across the plate with about 1 in. (2.5cm) hanging over the edge at each side.

2 Coat the first strip of paper with wallpaper paste or watered-down white glue and lay it in the mold, smoothing out any creases or air bubbles. Continue to lay pasted strips of paper across the plate, covering the edge of the last strip you have put in position with the new piece.

3 When you have completely covered the mold with the first layer of pasted paper, lay a second layer of strips across the plate, in the opposite direction to the first layer. This will guarantee that the papier-mâché is good and strong. Continue to cover the plate with layers of pasted paper in this way until you have completed eight layers. Then leave your plate to dry for 48 hours in a warm, dry place.

YOU WILL NEED

A plastic plate ● Petroleum jelly ● Paper ● Wallpaper paste or watered-down white glue ● Blunt knife or palette-knife ● Scissors ● Fine sandpaper ● Poster paints ● Black India ink ● Clear gloss varnish

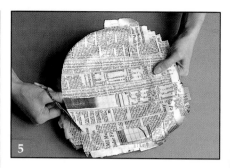

4 When the papier-mâché is dry, put the blade of a blunt knife or of a palette-knife under the edge of the paper where it meets the rim of the mold and gently prize it away. Because you greased the plastic plate with petroleum jelly, the paper should come away quite easily. Your paper shape will probably be a bit damp underneath, so lay it down in a warm place to dry for a few hours.

5 When the papier-mâché is dry, use a pair of scissors to trim the edge neatly back to within ¼ in. (5mm) of the rim.

6 The cut edge will need sealing. Take a strip of paper about 1 in. (2.5cm) wide, cover it with paste or glue and carefully wrap it over the edge, tearing it off at the other side. Repeat this process until you have sealed all around the edges of your plate. Leave the plate to dry overnight on a wire cake rack.

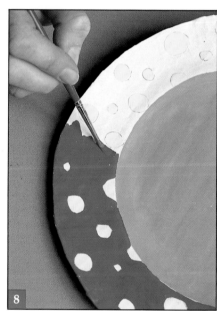

7 Rub down the dry plate gently with fine sandpaper, paying special attention to the sealed edge, which may be a bit lumpy. When it is smooth, give your plate two coats of white paint, allowing the first coat to dry before you add the second. Let the paint dry for an hour or so after the second coat is applied.

HELPFUL HINT . . .

Don't be tempted to leave papier-mâché to dry in strong sunlight – it may become warped.

8 Draw a design on the plate with pencil and start to fill in the color. You will probably have to use two layers of paint to get a good, deep color. Don't forget to paint the back as well!

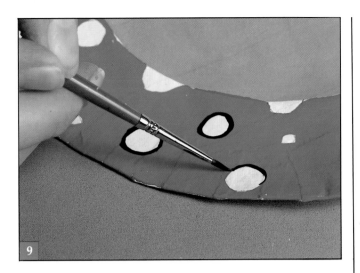

9 Allow your painted plate to dry for 4 hours and then outline your design with black India ink. Let the plate dry overnight.

10 Give the finished plate two coats of clear gloss varnish. You will probably have to paint the front of the plate and let it dry before you can varnish the back. Allow the first coat of varnish on each side of the plate to dry before you add the second. Remember to wash your varnishing brush with soap and water when you have finished.

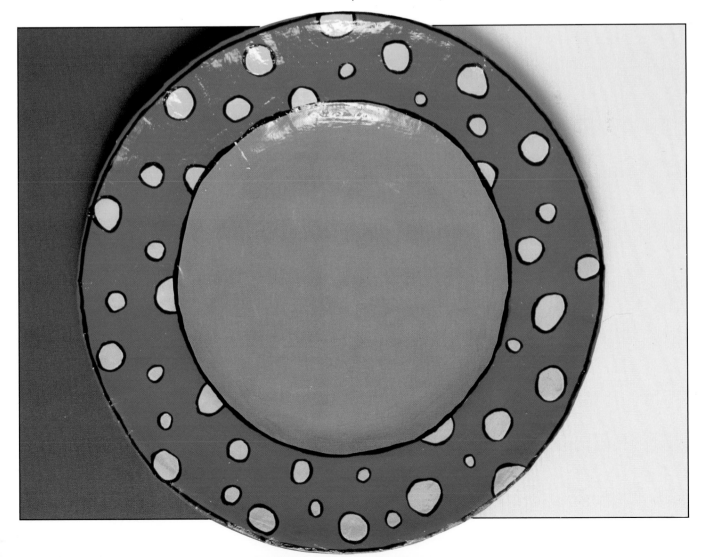

Barnacle Bowl

*In addition to using some of the basic techniques involved in making papier-mâché, this bowl is made from **two** separate pieces which have to be joined together. The main part of the bowl is made by laying thin strips of paper in a greased mold, while a smaller mold is used to make the "foot" that the bowl stands on. The bowl and foot are joined together with strips of papier-mâché, and their edges are bound with cord and covered to create a rim.*

YOU WILL NEED

Two plastic bowls, one about 8 in. (20cm) in diameter, one about 3 in. (7.5cm) in diameter • Petroleum jelly • Paper • Wallpaper paste or watered-down white glue • Blunt knife or palette-knife • Scissors • Preshrunk piping cord • Masking tape • White glue (undiluted) • Fine sandpaper • Poster paints • Black India ink • Clear gloss varnish

---

The body of the bowl illustrated is made in a plastic bowl with a diameter of about 8 in. (20cm), and the foot is made from a straight-sided margarine tub. Whatever bowls you choose, make sure that they look balanced together and as if they are meant to be joined.

The bowl is decorated with little pellets of paper pulp, which are applied in a regular pattern and painted in bright colors. Paper pulp is a very effective method of adding decoration to papier-mâché items, and quite ornate designs can be built up very quickly so that even rather plain shapes can be transformed into exciting articles.

The bowl can be used to hold a variety of dry objects, especially fruit, although you may want to choose varieties that don't clash with your color scheme! Don't keep wet things in it, however – it won't be waterproof, and you may spoil the varnished surface.

Making the bowl

1 Grease the insides of the molds with a little petroleum jelly so that the papier-mâché shapes can be easily removed when they are dry. Tear your paper into strips 1–1½ in. (2.5–4cm) wide and long enough to fit the bowl from one side to the other with about 1 in. (2.5cm) of excess paper on each edge. Begin to lay your pasted paper in the bowl, making sure that the strips lie flat against the walls. Continue to lay the paper in the bowl, covering the edge of the strip you have just put in place with the next strip. You may have to fan the strips out slightly as you move around the bowl so that the papier-mâché does not crease.

2 When you have finished the first layer of paper, start the second, laying the strips at right angles to the first layer, to give a good, strong bowl. Add eight layers of strips. Leave the papier-mâché to dry in a warm place for 48 hours.

3 When the surface of the bowl feels dry, gently insert the blade of a blunt knife or a palette-knife between the paper and mold, and ease the paper shells away from the sides. Lay the shape upside-down in a warm place to dry for a few hours.

4 The edges of your paper shapes will need sealing to stop them from coming apart. Use scissors to trim the excess paper back to within ¼ in. (5mm) of the edge of your bowl.

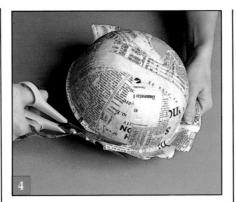

5 Then take a pasted strip of paper, about 1 in. (2.5cm) wide, and fully overlap the cut edge, tearing off the excess strip as you reach the back of the bowl each time. One layer of binding strips will be enough.

6 Leave the bound edges to dry and then place the piping cord around the outside edges of the bowl, pushing the cord right up against the lip of the rim. Secure the ends of the cord together with masking tape and tape the cord in place at several points around the rim. Then cover the cord with strips of paper, exactly as you did when you sealed the cut edges. Cover the cord with three layers of papier-mâché, and let the bowl dry for 24 hours.

Making the foot

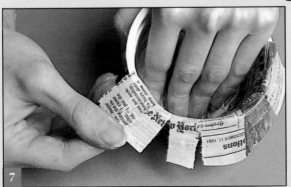

7 Grease the inside of the foot and lay in the strips of paper as you did in the bowl. Lay each of the 8 layers in at different angles to one another, and leave to dry out for 48 hours, before easing the paper cast out of the mold.

8 Trim back the paper as in step 4 and bind the edges with small pieces of paper. Leave to dry and then wrap the cord around the rim as in step 6. Secure it and seal with 3 layers of papier-mâché and allow it to dry for 24 hours.

Joining the foot to the bowl

9 Now dab some undiluted white glue on the top of the foot section and position it squarely under the body. Tape the two together with masking tape and leave the glue to dry for a couple of hours. Place a piece of cord around the join (a), tape it in place, and cover it with three layers of papier-mâché (b). Leave the bowl to dry for 24 hours.

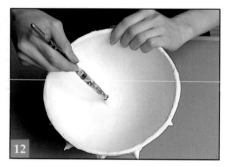

10 When your bowl is completely dry, you can make it more ornate with paper pulp additions if you wish. To make the "barnacles," take a strip of paper about 1 in. (2.5cm) wide and 8 in. (20cm) long. Coat it with glue and squash it into a pellet.

11 Then simply press the pellet firmly to the outside of your bowl to fix it, repeating the process as many times as you wish. If you want the "barnacles" to have a smooth surface, cover them with very short, thin strips of paper, say ¼ in. (5mm) wide and 1½ in. (4cm) long. Leave your bowl to dry for 24 hours.

12 When it is dry, smooth the bowl with fine sandpaper and paint it with two coats of white poster paint, allowing the first coat to dry thoroughly before adding the next.

13 Paint the rope bands in colors that contrast with the body – you will probably need two coats of color to cover the white paint completely – then paint the "barnacles" in whatever colors appeal to you.

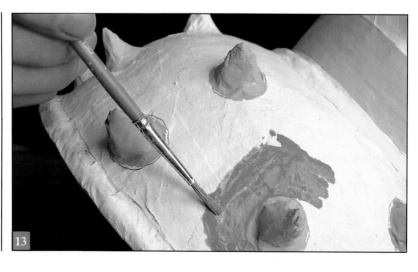

14 Let the paint dry for 3–4 hours and paint contrasting black ink lines on your bowl using a fine paint-brush. Leave the bowl to dry for 24 hours.

15 Give your bowl two coats of clear gloss varnish, allowing the first coat to dry thoroughly before adding the second. Remember to clean your varnishing brush with soap and water when you have finished.

JEWELRY

Lots of different kinds of jewelry can be made in papier-mâché – small, neat brooches and earrings as well as over-the-top necklaces and bangle bracelets. Make a selection and wear them according to your mood! All the items shown here involve the basic papier-mâché techniques, and you can make some stunning pieces by combining methods. Papier-mâché jewelry will make lovely presents for birthdays, Christmas, Mother's Day, or any special occasion, and your family and friends will be thrilled to receive something made especially for them.

You can, of course, personalize jewelry. You could write your name or a special message on a brooch or decorate bracelets and necklaces to match special outfits or costumes. The possibilities are endless – have fun trying some of them!

You will need what are known as "findings" for some of your jewelry. Findings are what you use to finish a piece – brooch pins, earring clips, necklace fastenings, and so on. They are inexpensive and can be bought from craft and hobby stores and from jewelry suppliers. If you are making earrings for pierced ears and are allergic to metal, you can buy silver and gold hooks, although these are more expensive.

Earrings

These bright flower earrings look very attractive, and their design matches the daisy necklace featured later in this section, so you could make a set by decorating both pieces in the same way. Although they are quite large, these earrings are very light, and you could make them even larger or longer without weighing your ears down. Other motifs that would look good include hearts, stars, and fish. You could make several pairs when you have learned the basic technique. The earrings are attached to the ears by clips, which are stuck to the backs of the yellow disks with strong glue.

EARRINGS TEMPLATES *(Thin cardboard)*

Making the earrings

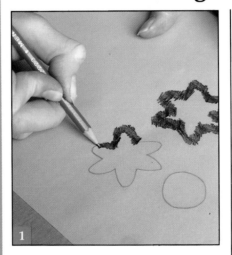

1 Trace the earring shapes from the pattern above and transfer them to the thin cardboard.

2 Cut around the shapes with a craft knife or scissors. **Ask an adult to help you if you use a craft knife, because it will have a very sharp blade.** Paint your cutout shapes with one coat of watered-down white glue. Lay them on a wire cake rack for 4 hours to dry.

YOU WILL NEED

Tracing paper ● Thin cardboard approximately 4 x 4 in. (10 x 10cm) ● Craft knife or scissors ● Wallpaper paste or watered-down white glue ● Paper ● Fine sandpaper ● Poster paints ● Black India ink ● Clear gloss varnish ● Darning needle ● White glue (undiluted) ● 2 pairs of earring hooks and eyes ● Strong, clear glue ● 1 pair of clip fastenings ● Small pair of pliers

HELPFUL HINT . . .

Knives, especially craft knives, can be dangerous. Always hold what you are cutting very carefully, and cut away from you. Better still, ask an adult to help you.

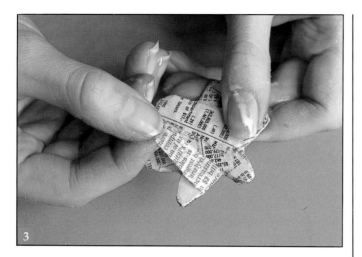

3 Using small strips of paper, about ½ in. × 2 in. (12mm × 5cm), cover the earring shapes with three layers of pasted paper. Work carefully around each petal, making sure that your papier-mâché does not become too lumpy so that it will have a smooth finish. Lay the papered shapes on a cake rack to dry for 24 hours.

4 When the shapes are completely dry, smooth them down lightly with fine sandpaper and coat them with two layers of white paint, allowing the first to dry before you add the second. Draw the center of the daisy on your flower shapes. The petal outlines and swirls will be drawn freehand on top of the poster paint later with black India ink.

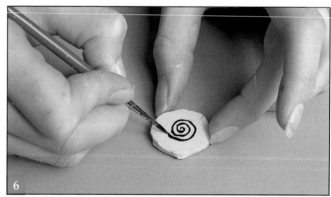

5 Start to fill in the color. The petals were painted light blue, and then, when this coat was dry, they were painted again in violet, with the light blue allowed to show through in patches. The disks have been given two coats of yellow paint.

When you have painted all the pieces, allow them to dry for 4 hours.

6 Then, using a fine paintbrush, carefully draw in the black outlines and swirls. Let the earrings dry overnight, then varnish the fronts with clear gloss varnish. Lay the pieces (varnished side up!) on a wire cake rack to dry. Varnish the backs and allow them to dry again. Repeat the process so that the fronts and backs have two coats of varnish.

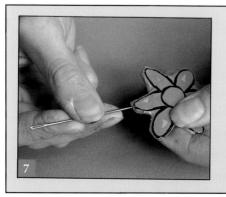

7 When the second coat of varnish is dry, make a small hole with a darning needle in the top of the petal section and in the bottom of the disk. Dab a little undiluted white glue into the holes. Push an earring hook section into the hole in each flower and an eye into each disk.

8 Dab some strong, clear glue onto the earring clips, and position one on the back of each disk. Press the disk and clip together firmly, and let all the earring pieces dry overnight.

9 Loop the hook into the eye, joining the disk and the flower, and close the opening with a small pair of pliers. Your earrings are now ready to wear!

Bracelets

Bracelets can be as simple or as ornate as you like. They can be made for special occasions and decorated accordingly, or they can be worn as bright, cheerful, everyday accessories. Here are two simple examples for you to make, which can be adapted to any occasion. You might like a perfectly plain circle, decorated with vibrant patterns and color, or you might prefer a more sophisticated, but simply decorated, bracelet.

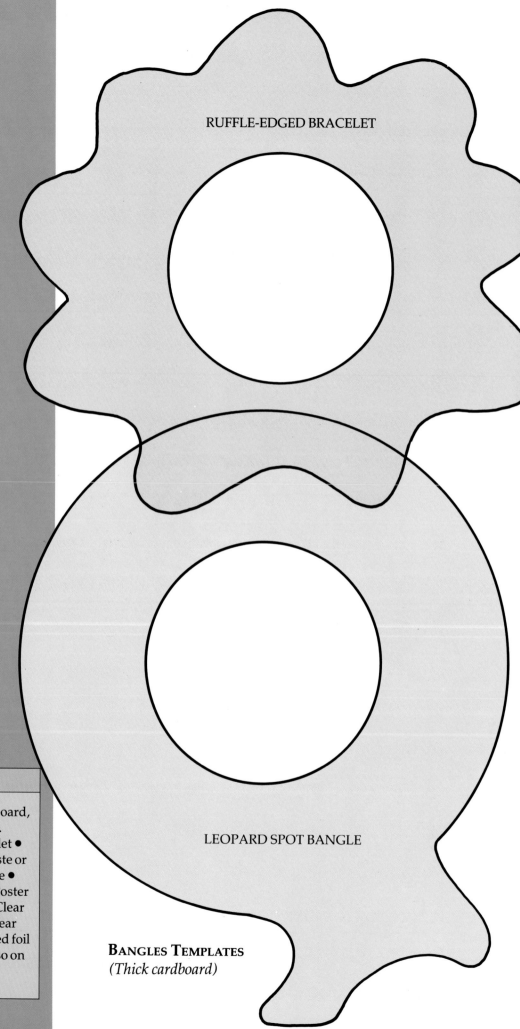

RUFFLE-EDGED BRACELET

LEOPARD SPOT BANGLE

BANGLES TEMPLATES
(Thick cardboard)

YOU WILL NEED

Tracing paper • Thick cardboard, approximately 8 × 8 in. (20 × 20cm) for each bracelet • Craft knife • Wallpaper paste or watered-down white glue • Paper • Fine sandpaper • Poster paints • Black India ink • Clear gloss varnish • Strong, clear glue • Small pieces of colored foil from sweet wrappers and so on

You could paint your bangle bracelet in one color all over and apply fake gemstones for a glittery, sumptuous effect. You could use small pieces of mirror tile, but be very careful not to cut yourself on the sharp edges! Paper pulp can be added to give extra interest to plain shapes.

Remember that you could also make a bracelet using the same method as the daisy necklace in this section. The modelling-clay shapes will have to be smaller, however, so that the resulting beads are in scale with your hand!

Making your bracelets

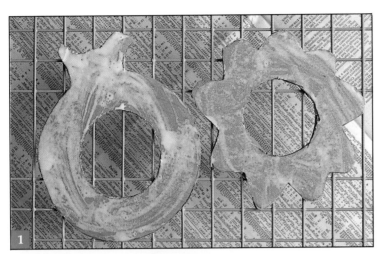

1 Trace the shape you prefer from the patterns in the book and transfer it to the cardboard. Cut around the shape with a craft knife and cut a hand hole in the middle – ask an adult to help you with the cutting. If you are making the ruffle-edged bangle, cut quite precisely around your pattern so that you get a nice smooth edge. Give the bracelet shape a coat of watered-down white glue, and leave it to dry for 4 hours on a wire cake rack.

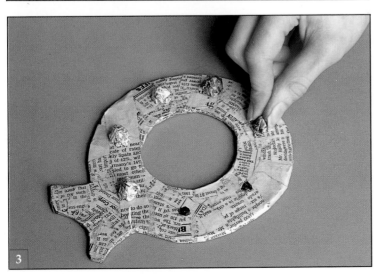

2 When it is dry, cover the cardboard shape with three layers of pasted paper. Because it is more complicated to cover a curved surface than a straight one, you will have to pay special attention to overlapping the paper smoothly, especially around the inside of the bracelet, where the curve is quite pronounced. Take a little time, and use small, thin pieces of paper. When you have finished papering your bracelet, leave it to dry on a wire cake rack for 24 hours.

3 Smooth the surface of the bangle lightly with fine sandpaper. At this stage, you can add decorative details in paper pulp if you want to. To make the spots on the leopard bangle, mark six equally spaced dots around the bangle. Take a strip of paper, 1 in. (2.5cm) wide and 4–5 in. (10–12.5cm) long, cover both sides with paste or glue, and roll it up into a little ball between your fingers. Press the pellet on the first of your dots and continue the process until all the dots are covered. Leave the bangle to dry on a wire cake rack for 24 hours.

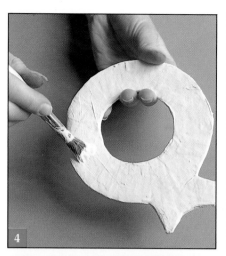

4 When the bangle has dried, sand it lightly and apply two coats of white paint, allowing the first coat to dry before you add the second. The basic shapes can be decorated in many ways.

5 Draw the design on the bangle and start to apply the colors.

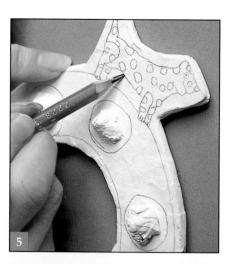

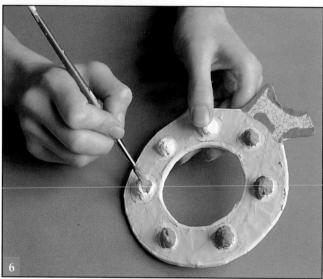

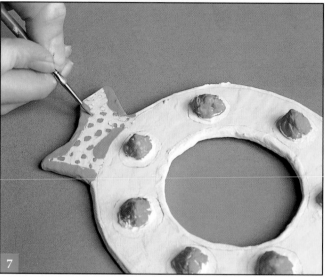

6 The leopard bangle is painted in yellow and dark brown to echo the appearance of the animal's skin.

7 Apply a second layer of paint so that the white paint doesn't show through.

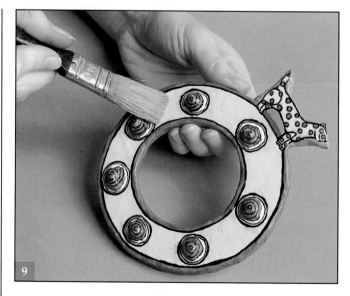

8 Fill in the details, and then, using a fine brush, paint in the black outlines with India ink.

9 Let the bangle dry for 24 hours; then give it two coats of clear gloss varnish.

Ruffle-edged bangle

10 The ruffle-edged bangle is painted in one color. When the paint was dry, it was given a coat of clear gloss varnish and left again to dry. To add the decorations shown in the photograph, spread clear glue on each "petal," and add bits of colored foil from candy wrappers to make interesting patterns. When the glue has dried, decorate the other side of the bangle in the same way. Apply a final coat of clear gloss varnish over the top of the colored foil, and leave the bangle bracelet to dry for 24 hours before you wear it.

Necklace

Exciting jewelry is very simple to make in papier-mâché, and because it is so light, you can wear enormous pieces without being weighed down!

This necklace has been painted in bright, cheerful colors, but you could, of course, paint the beads in a subtler way to achieve a more sophisticated effect. A necklace made entirely of papier-mâché beads is very attractive, but you could alternate colorful wooden, clay, or glass beads with the papier-mâché ones.

The cutout daisy has been added to give a focal point to the necklace. You can use any motif you like.

YOU WILL NEED

Modeling clay, about 1lb. (500g) ● Paper ● Wallpaper paste or watered-down white glue ● Tracing paper ● Thin cardboard, approximately 4 × 4 in. (10 × 10cm) ● Scissors ● Craft knife ● Palette-knife ● White glue (undiluted) ● Masking tape ● Fine sandpaper ● Poster paints ● Black India ink ● Clear gloss varnish ● Darning needle ● Metal eye with ¼ in. (0.5cm) screw shank ● Round black elastic, 16 in. (70cm) ● Spacer beads (optional)

HELPFUL HINT . . .

When you are modeling with clay, roll it between the palms of your hands for a few minutes until it becomes soft enough to be molded. If it is a very hot day, on the other hand, and your clay is too soft, put it in the fridge for an hour or so until it has hardened up again.

Making the necklace

1 Roll small pieces of clay into balls, gradually increasing the size from 1 in. (2.5cm) to 1½ in. (4cm) in diameter. Tear small, thin strips of paper, approximately ½ × 2 in. (12mm × 5cm), paste them and start to cover the clay balls. Try to overlap the edges of the strips neatly.

2 When you have covered each ball with five layers, roll them gently between the palms of your hands to smooth the edges. Leave the beads to dry on a wire cake rack for 48 hours.

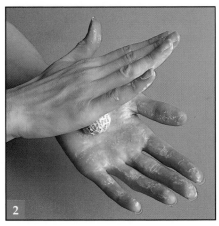

3 Meanwhile, trace the flower motif from the diagram in the book, and transfer it to thin cardboard. Cut around the flower with scissors and paint it with a coat of watered-down white glue to minimize the risk of warping. Let it dry for 2–3 hours, then cover it with three layers of papier-mâché, using small, thin pieces of paper to go around the petals. Leave the flower to dry on a wire cake rack for 24 hours.

4 When the beads are dry enough, carefully cut them in half with a craft knife. **Ask an adult to help you do this.** Leave the opened beads for an hour or so before you remove the clay. This will allow the cut edges to harden slightly and lessen the chances of the papier-mâché tearing when you pull out the clay.

5 Gently prize the clay from the paper casts with the blade of a palette-knife. Let the empty casts dry for 12 hours.

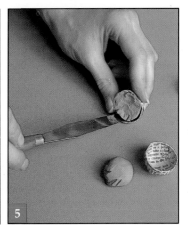

6 When they are dry, smear a little undiluted white glue along the cut edges of each bead and join the halves back together, holding the joins firmly with small pieces of masking tape. Let the glue set slightly, and then, without removing the masking tape, seal the beads with small, thin pieces of papier-mâché. One layer of paper across the joins will be sufficient. Let the beads dry for 24 hours.

7 When the beads and flower motif are dry, smooth their surfaces lightly with fine sandpaper. Give all the pieces two coats of white paint, allowing each coat to dry properly before you apply the next.

8 You are now ready to decorate your necklace. It is up to you how elaborate you make it. This one has been simply decorated, using bright, cheerful colors. First, each bead was painted with a light color. Then, when the paint was dry, a second coat of paint was added. You can use a darker shade of the first color or another color that complements it. Here, the color of the first coat of paint has been allowed to show through the second, and this gives a pleasing mottled effect to the bead.

9 The flower is painted in two colors, chosen to reflect those used for the beads. Again, the petals of the flower have been painted in two shades of the same color, and the lighter shade allowed to show through from underneath. This gives a livelier effect than one flat color, although you may prefer just one shade of pink. Whichever effect you choose, apply two coats of paint, allowing each coat to dry thoroughly before you add the second.

10 When the colors are dry, you can add black ink lines for definition. Swirls of ink have been painted on the beads to emphasize their shape. You will probably have to paint half the bead and let the ink dry for a few minutes before finishing it underneath; otherwise, you might smudge your lines. The daisy has been simply outlined with ink and the shape of its petals defined. Allow the paint to dry for 24 hours.

11 Give each piece of your necklace two coats of clear gloss varnish, allowing the first coat to dry thoroughly before you add the second one. As with the paint, you might find it best to let the beads dry on one side before you varnish the other, to stop them from sticking to your work surface.

12 To assemble the necklace, use a darning needle to make a hole in the top of the daisy motif. Dab a little white glue in the hole and gently screw the metal eye into it. Thread the darning needle with the round elastic and tie a knot in one end. You may need an adult to help you with the next stage. Take a papier-mâché bead and carefully push the needle through the center and out the other side.

13 Pull the elastic through and then, if you are using them, add two spacer beads, followed by another papier-mâché bead. When you have strung half the papier-mâché beads on the elastic, add the daisy motif, which will hang from the elastic by its metal eye, and finish stringing the rest of the beads. Cut the elastic after the last bead, leaving approximately 2 in. (5cm) extra. Tie the two ends of elastic firmly together, and your necklace is ready to wear.

Brooch

This flapping chicken makes a simple, bright brooch, and its bold colors will brighten up your jacket or sweater.

The brooch shape is cut from cardboard and covered with three layers of small papier-mâché strips. The fish shapes in the mobile described later in this book would also make good brooches, as would the flower motif from the necklace.

BROOCH TEMPLATE (*Thick cardboard*)

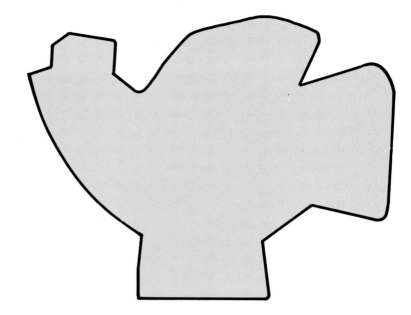

Making the brooch

1 Trace the outline of the chicken from the diagram in the book and transfer it to the thin cardboard. Cut out the chicken with scissors and give it a coat of watered-down PVA adhesive. Lay it on a wire cake rack to dry for 4 hours.

2 Take the cardboard shape and start to cover it with pasted paper. Use small, thin strips of paper, about ½ × 3 in. (12mm × 7.5cm). Try to keep the papier-mâché smooth around the edges so that the brooch will look nicer when it is painted. Apply three layers of papier-mâché, and leave it to dry on a wire cake rack for 24 hours.

3 Smooth the surface of the dry chicken shape with fine sandpaper, and give it two coats of white poster paint, allowing the first coat to dry thoroughly before you add the second.

4 Let the white paint dry thoroughly and draw on the chicken's features in pencil

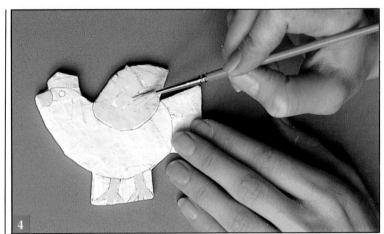

5 Fill in the design with color. You will probably need to use two coats of paint to achieve a good deep color.

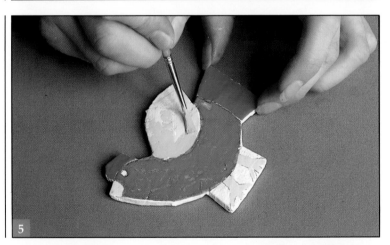

6 Let the paint dry for 4 hours and then paint in the black outline in India ink. Let the brooch dry overnight. Give the brooch two coats of clear gloss varnish, allowing the first coat to dry properly before you add the second. Remember to clean your varnishing brush in soapy water when you have finished.

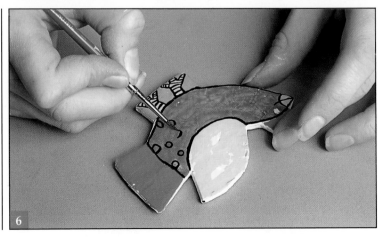

7 Allow the varnish to dry thoroughly; then smear strong, clear glue on the back of the brooch pin.

8 Position it centrally on the back of your brooch, about one-third of the way down, and press it firmly into place. Leave to dry for 24 hours before you wear your brooch.

BOXES

There is a long tradition of making boxes with papier-mâché, especially in the Kashmir region of India, where very solid little pill boxes and trinket chests are produced. They are often beautifully decorated with scenes of horsemen and animals, and flowers are also a favorite motif. The Kashmiri boxes are made from many layers of paper, which are pounded to compress them, and dried in the sun.

The boxes featured in this section are similar in spirit to those of India, but they are made of cardboard which is covered with layers of papier-mâché. The pen and pencil holder, although not strictly a box, has been included in this section because it is used to store or hold objects – the traditional function of boxes. The other boxes are simple in structure, and they close in different ways. One has a fabric hinge along the back, while one has a lid with a "lip" underneath, which fits snugly into the body of the box.

Boxes can, of course, be as large or as small as your want, and they can be made to any design that you please. You could make one with lots of small compartments to store your treasures or perhaps a "double decker," with two levels for letters and stationery. You could also fashion special "packaging" boxes for Christmas presents and birthdays. Not only would they last a long time and be reusable, but you wouldn't need to buy wrapping paper!

Jeweled Box

This little box is decorated very simply and effectively with silver foil and glass "gemstones," and it employs another way of decorating papier-mâché. Sequins would be a good alternative to gemstones, and you could, of course, use different colored foil or perhaps self-adhesive decorative paper to cover the box.

YOU WILL NEED

Thick cardboard, approximately 13 × 11 in. (33 × 28cm) ● Craft knife ● White glue (undiluted) ● Masking tape ● Wallpaper paste or watered-down white glue ● Paper ● Fine sandpaper ● Silver foil ● Strong, clear glue ● Glass "gemstones" in assorted colors

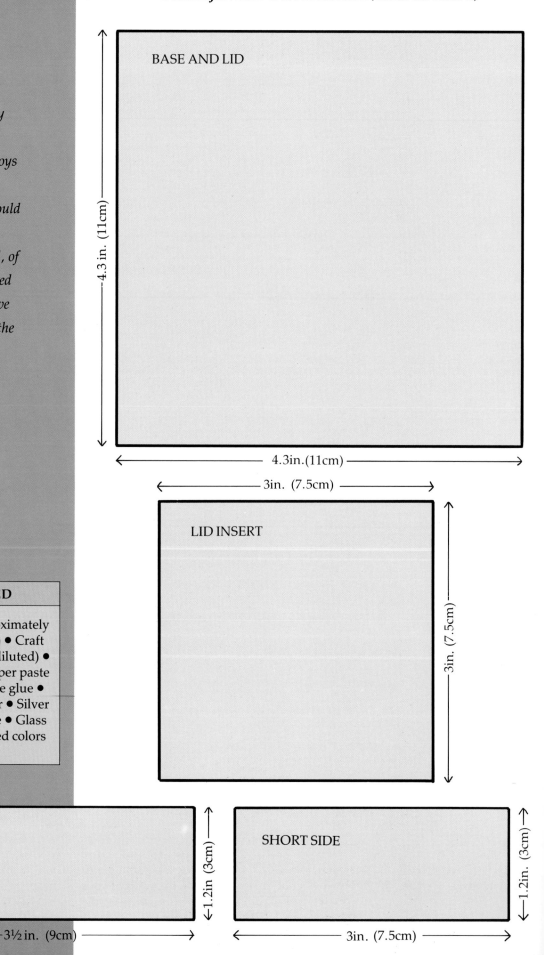

SMALL JEWELED BOX TEMPLATE *(Thick cardboard)*

BASE AND LID

4.3 in. (11cm)

4.3in.(11cm)

3in. (7.5cm)

LID INSERT

3in. (7.5cm)

LONG SIDE

1.2in (3cm)

3½ in. (9cm)

SHORT SIDE

1.2in. (3cm)

3in. (7.5cm)

Making the jeweled box

1 Measure the dimensions from the diagrams opposite and transfer them to the cardboard. Cut them out and form a square out of the wall pieces, holding the pieces together with masking tape. Cover the underside of the walls with white glue and stick the rectangle squarely onto the box base, securing it with masking tape. Then glue the lid insert onto the underside of the lid, holding it in place with tape. Leave everything to dry for a few hours and then give both sections a coat of watered-down PVA. Leave to dry out overnight.

2 Cover both pieces of the box with three layers of papier-mâché. Use strips of paper approximately 1 in. (2.5cm) wide. When you have finished papering, leave the box to dry for 24 hours on a wire cake rack.

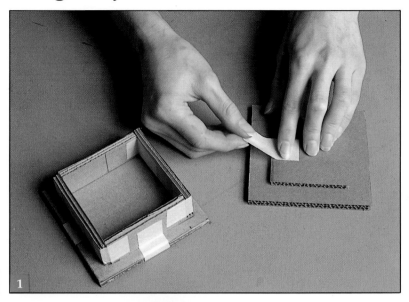

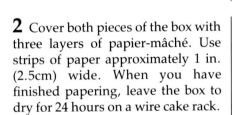

3 Lightly sand the surfaces of your dry box with fine sandpaper and give it one coat of white poster paint. Although you will not see this paint, it will make it easier to apply the foil, which will show up better against white paint than newsprint. Let the paint dry for 3–4 hours.

4 When the paint is dry, the box is ready to be covered in foil. The easiest way is to use long, thin pieces of foil to go around the walls of your box, and large pieces to cover the lid, base, and inside of your box. Cut all the pieces of foil to size before you start gluing it in place. As foil will mold itself to the shape of your box, it is a good idea to fit all the pieces of foil around your box as a trial to make sure they are the right shape and size. Use strong, clear glue to stick the foil down.

5 Once you have glued the foil to your box, leave it to dry for an hour or so before you add the "gem-stones." Give some thought to the pattern you want to create, and try a few variations before you glue the stones down permanently. When you have decided on the arrange-ment, smear a little strong, clear glue on the underside of each stone, and press it firmly onto the box. Let the box dry for 24 hours before you use it.

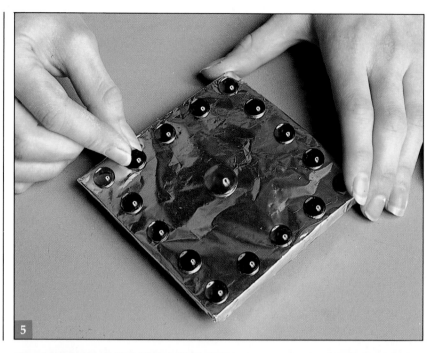

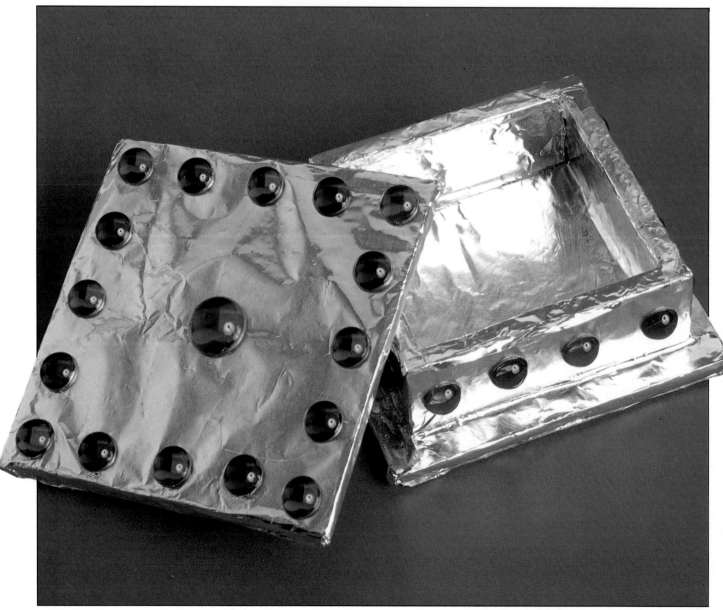

Pen and Pencil Tray

This pen and pencil tray could also be used to hold a multitude of other useful things – scissors, paperclips, and erasers, for example – to help you to keep your desk neat. You could make it to keep sewing things in, or use it as a holder for your paints and brushes. If you made the sides higher, it would hold stationery. Add more compartments or make it bigger to suit your particular hobbies, and decorate it accordingly. You could even make several and build up a stacking system for yourself!

YOU WILL NEED

Thick corrugated cardboard, approximately 17 × 15 in. (43 × 38cm) ● Craft knife ● White glue (undiluted) ● Masking tape ● Wallpaper paste or watered-down white glue ● Paper ● Fine sandpaper ● Poster paints ● Clear gloss varnish

PENCIL TRAY TEMPLATE *(Thick cardboard)*

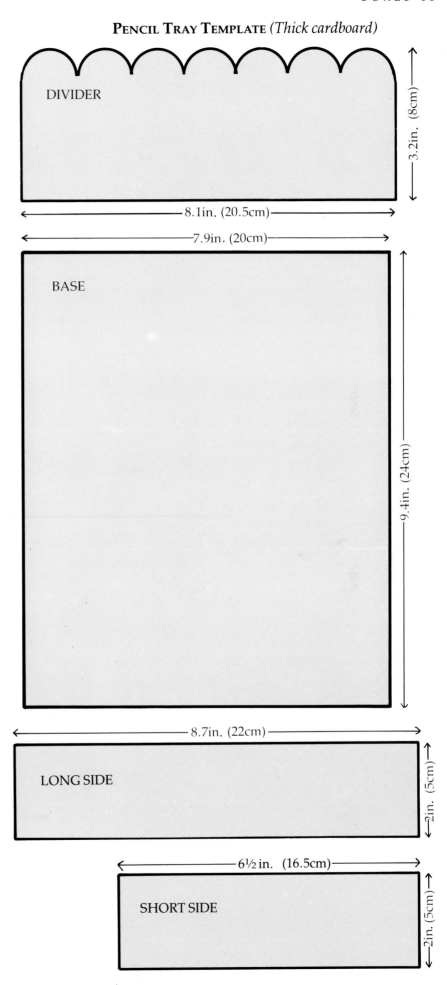

DIVIDER

3.2in. (8cm)

8.1in. (20.5cm)

7.9in. (20cm)

BASE

9.4in. (24cm)

8.7in. (22cm)

LONG SIDE

2in. (5cm)

6½ in. (16.5cm)

SHORT SIDE

2in. (5cm)

Making the tray

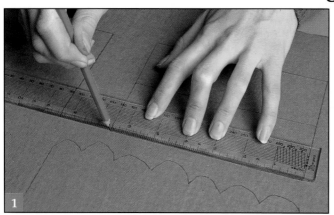

1 Draw the shapes for the base, sides, and divider from the diagram in the book on the cardboard, making sure that you transfer the measurements accurately.

2 Ask an adult to help you cut out the shapes with a craft knife; the blade will be very sharp. Cut the cardboard against a metal ruler.

3 Take the four pieces of cardboard that make up the sides of your pencil tray and glue them together at right angles with undiluted white glue to form a rectangle. Hold the joints securely with masking tape. Smear a little glue along the underside of the joined sides, and place them on the base. When correctly positioned, secure them firmly with masking tape.

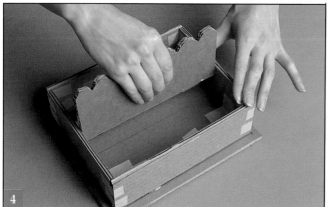

4 Squeeze a line of white glue on the underside and sides of the wavy-edged divider, and position it down the center of the tray. Secure it with masking tape.

5 Now paint the whole tray with watered-down glue, and leave it to dry for 4 hours.

6 When it is dry, cover the tray with three layers of papier-mâché. Use thin, long strips of paper, about 1 × 6 in. (2.5 × 15cm). Take care to push the paper well into the inside corners to give a sharp, smooth look. Use smaller pieces of paper, approximately ½ × 2 in. (12mm × 5cm), to cover the wavy-edged divider, as this will keep it from becoming too lumpy and uneven. Leave the tray to dry for 24 hours.

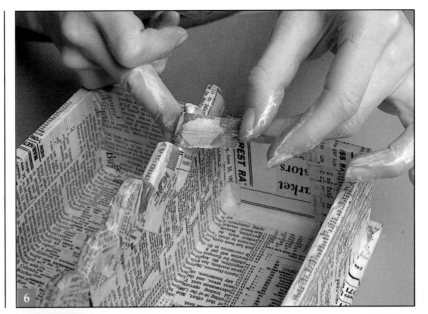

7 When the tray is dry, sand all its surfaces lightly with fine sandpaper and give it two coats of white poster paint, letting each coat dry properly before you add the next. Draw your decoration on the tray. The one illustrated is painted with pictures of the items it might hold – pens, pencils, scissors, and paintbrushes. You might like to use this idea for your tray, or you might want to have an overall design of dots or stripes, executed in contrasting colors, or to write your name in fancy lettering.

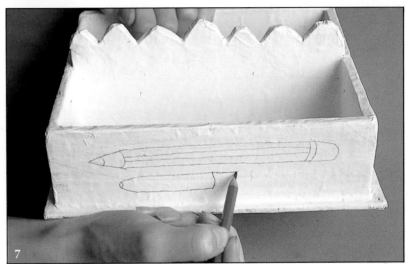

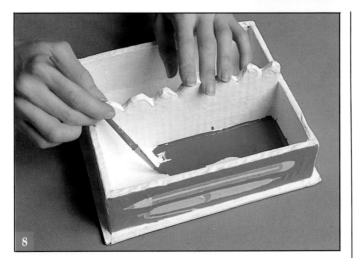

8 When you have drawn in the designs, fill them in with your chosen colors. Remember that the underside of the base will need to be decorated, too.

9 You will need to apply two coats of paint to achieve a good, dense covering, but do not add the second coat until the first one is completely dry. When you have finished painting your tray, outline your design with black India ink.

10 Let your tray dry overnight, and then give it two coats of clear gloss varnish, allowing the first to dry before applying the second. Remember to clean your brush thoroughly with soap and water when you have finished varnishing.

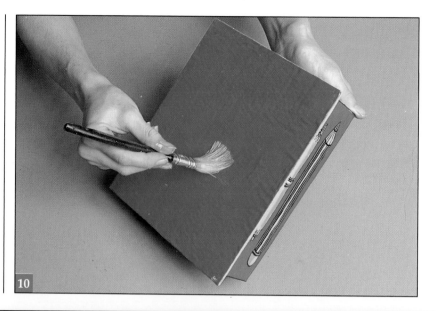

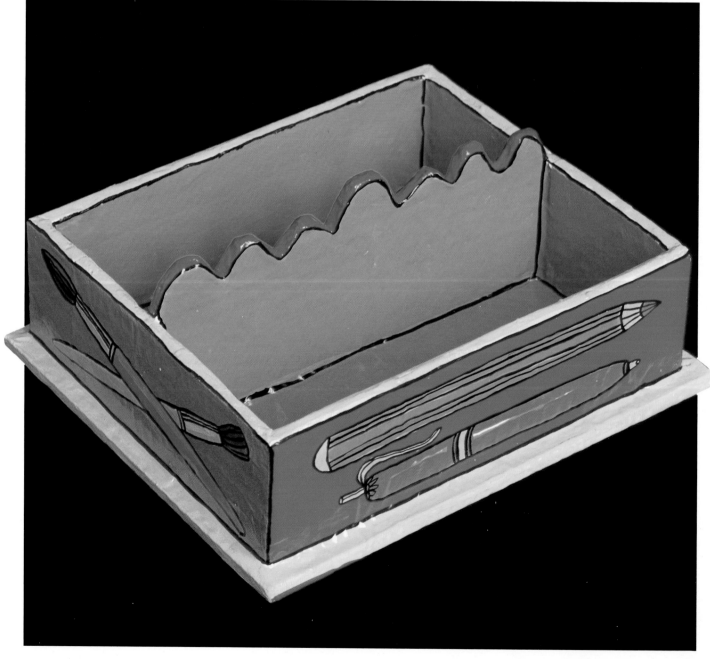

Hinged Box

This box, which closes with a hinged lid, is decorated with a technique known as découpage. This involves collecting interesting scraps from such sources as magazines, newspapers, and greeting cards. The cutout scraps are stuck onto objects as a decoration and varnished in place.

This box has been decorated with black and white engravings that were photocopied from an old encyclopedia, but almost anything that you like would be suitable.

YOU WILL NEED

Thick cardboard, approximately 16 × 14 in. (40 × 36cm) ● Craft knife ● White glue (undiluted) ● Masking tape ● Wallpaper paste or watered-down white glue ● Paper ● Fine sandpaper ● Cotton ribbon, 1 in. (2.5cm) wide and 4 in. (10cm) long ● An assortment of scraps cut from newspapers, magazines, greeting cards, wallpaper books, etc. ● Clear gloss varnish

HINGED BOX TEMPLATE *(Thick cardboard)*

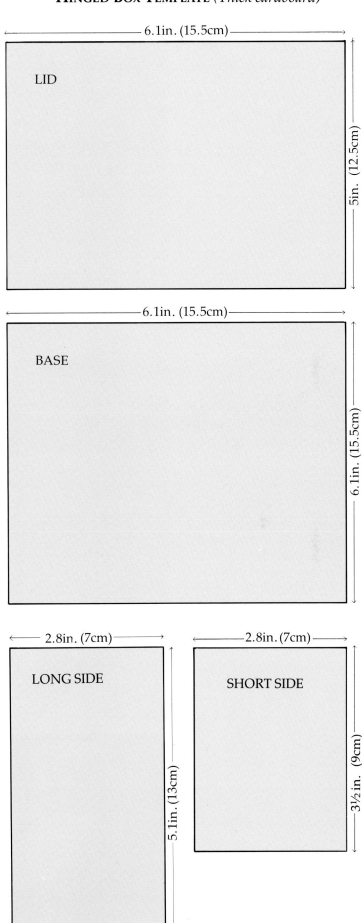

6.1in. (15.5cm)

LID

5in. (12.5cm)

6.1in. (15.5cm)

BASE

6.1in. (15.5cm)

2.8in. (7cm)

LONG SIDE

5.1in. (13cm)

2.8in. (7cm)

SHORT SIDE

3½in. (9cm)

Making the hinged box

1 Accurately transfer the measurements for each piece of the box from the diagram in the book onto the cardboard. Ask an adult to cut each piece out for you with a craft knife and metal ruler. Take the pieces of cardboard that make up the sides and smear the edges with white glue. Join them at right angles and secure the joins firmly with masking tape.

2 Give all the pieces of the box a coat of watered-down white glue and leave them to dry for 4 hours on a wire cake rack. Cover the underside of the joined side section with white glue, and place it squarely on the base. Tape the joins together with masking tape. Leave the glue to set for an hour or so, and then cover the box pieces with three layers of papier-mâché. Let them dry overnight on a wire cake rack.

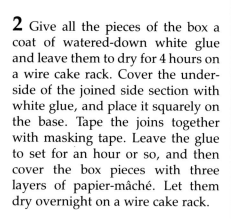

3 When the papier-mâché is dry, smooth it down with fine sandpaper. Fold the piece of ribbon in two along its length and coat half its width with undiluted glue. Press the glued ribbon along the back top edge of the box body. Put glue on the other half of the ribbon, and press it onto the box lid. You will probably have to support the lid on a pile of magazines or one or two books while the glue dries. Cover the edges of the ribbon hinge with two layers of papier-mâché, avoiding the crease along the center, and let it rest on its support for 24 hours.

4 When it is completely dry, lightly sand the extra papier-mâché around the hinge and give the whole box two coats of white poster paint.

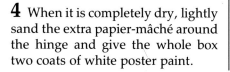

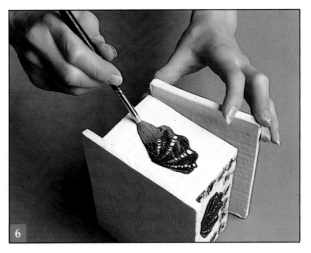

5 Let the paint dry thoroughly, and then start to arrange your cutout scraps, trying out several designs before you glue them down. Use a little undiluted glue to stick the scraps to the box, and leave them to dry for a few hours in a warm place.

6 If you are leaving some of the box surface white, use watered-down glue, but not too much, as a varnish, since clear gloss varnish tends to look slightly yellow on top of white. Otherwise, use clear gloss varnish. Whichever you use, give your box two coats, allowing the first coat to dry thoroughly before you apply the second. Leave your box to dry for 24 hours before you use it.

Heart-shaped Box

This box is decorated with pieces of colored foil from candy wrappers. It is fairly simple to make in spite of its shape and can be used to contain a variety of small objects including jewelry, money, and candy. It would make a pretty gift, especially for Valentine's Day!

HEART-SHAPED BOX TEMPLATE *(Thick and thin cardboard)*

BASE AND LID *(Thick cardboard)*

Guide line for box wall

1.2 in.

12.6 in. (32cm)

(3cm)

BOX SIDE *(Thin cardboard)*

LID INSERT *(Thick cardboard)*

YOU WILL NEED

Tracing paper • Thick corrugated cardboard, approximately 12 × 10 in. (30.4 × 25.4cm) • Thin corrugated cardboard, approximately 14 × 2 in. (35.5 × 5cm) • Craft knife • White glue (undiluted) • Masking tape • Strong, clear glue • Wallpaper paste or watered-down white glue • Paper • Fine sandpaper • Poster paints • Clear gloss varnish • Small pieces of colored foil

Making the heart-shaped box

1 Trace the shapes from the diagram in the book, transferring the outlines for the base and top to the thick cardboard and the outline for the side to the thin cardboard. You should lay it to the card so that the corrugations run vertically, which will make it easier to curve the shape as it is being stuck down. Cut out all the box pieces. **Ask an adult to help you as you will need to use a craft knife, and its blade will be very sharp.** Take the length of thin card that will form the box side. Bend it gently along its length at every corrugation so that it curves easily as you stick it along the guideline on the base. Coat the underside edge of the box wall with white glue, and glue it carefully along the guideline. Secure it every 1–1½ in. (2.5–4cm) with masking tape.

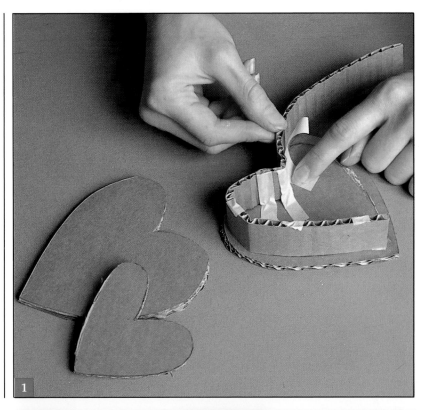

2 Place the lid insert centrally on the back of the lid. Draw a pencil line around it, and cover the back of the lid insert with strong, clear glue. Press it back on the lid inside the pencil line. Leave the lid and the base to dry for an hour or so, and then give both pieces a coat of watered-down white glue. Leave both pieces to dry for about 4 hours in a warm place.

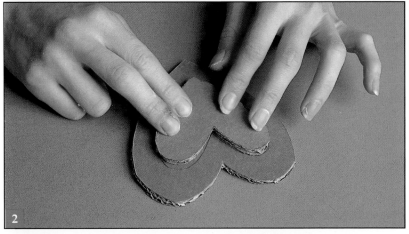

3 Cover both pieces with two layers of papier-mâché and leave them to dry for 24 hours on a wire cake rack.

4 When both parts of the box are dry, smooth them lightly with fine sandpaper and give them two coats of white poster paint, allowing the first coat to dry before you add the second.

5 Paint the lid and outside of your box with two coats of red poster paint, remembering to let the first coat dry completely before you add the second.

6 Give the inside of the box two coats of paint; the inside of the box illustrated here has been painted yellow, but you can use any color you like. Let the paint dry thoroughly, and then varnish the box with one layer of clear gloss varnish. Leave the box to dry for 24 hours.

7 When the varnish is dry, you can begin to glue the decorations on. Cut out pieces of foil and use strong, clear glue to glue them to the varnished surface of the box. Your pattern can be as flamboyant or as simple as you like. You may want to line the box with foil, too.

8 Allow the box to dry overnight and then varnish carefully over the foil additions, taking care not to lift them off with your brush. Let the first layer of varnish dry thoroughly and then add another. As always, clean your brush in soap and water when you have finished with it.

FRAMES

Simple frames for pictures and photographs are quite easy to make and can be decorated in a variety of ways. They can be made especially for a particular picture or photograph, with the frame echoing or embellishing the image, or they can be more general in appearance so they look good with a variety of pictures.

You can use all kinds of things to decorate your frame – broken pieces of pottery arranged to create a mosaic effect, brightly colored foil from candy wrappers, sequins, buttons, shells, glass "gemstones," and so on. The frames featured here are finished off with gilt disks and pebbles found on the seashore. You can choose the idea that most appeals, or you might like to combine two or three ideas in one frame.

The frames described here close in different ways. The heart-shaped frame is sealed, and its contents are permanently enclosed.

The frame with the heart-shaped opening is hinged on one side and fastens with a bow.

Heart-shaped Frame

This is a permanently sealed frame, so you will have to decide carefully what to put inside it before you make it. It is decorated with two different sizes of gilt coins – the kind that are sewn on scarves and costumes – and they give it a sumptuous appearance. There is no need to buy things to decorate it, though; old brass and gilt buttons would look just as good, especially if you used several different sizes and colors.

The picture of the sun has been enclosed in the frame because it is so cheerful, but you might like to put in a special photograph instead. Because you won't be able to remove it once the frame is sealed, you might prefer to make a color photocopy of your picture and keep the original. The contents of the frame are protected by a small piece of acetate, which keeps dust and dirt from settling on the picture.

Making the heart-shaped frame

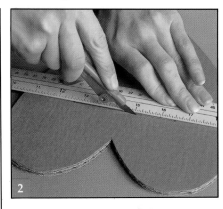

1 Draw a large heart on the thick cardboard. Make it about 10 in. (25cm) long from top to bottom and 8 in. (20cm) across at its widest point. Trace the shape of this heart exactly on the tracing paper and transfer it to the thinner card. Ask an adult to help you cut around the heart shapes with a craft knife.

2 Use a ruler to draw a rectangle approximately 4 in. (10cm) wide and 2¾ in. (7cm) high in the center of the thick cardboard. This will be the opening of your frame. Ask an adult to help you with the craft knife. Coat both pieces of cardboard with watered-down glue and dry them for 4 hours on a wire cake rack.

YOU WILL NEED

Thick cardboard, approximately 12 × 10 in. (30 × 25cm) ● Tracing paper ● Thin cardboard, approximately 12 × 10 in. (30 × 25cm) ● Craft knife ● Wallpaper paste or watered-down white glue ● Paper ● Fine sandpaper ● Acetate, 4½ × 3½ in. (11 × 8cm) ● Strong, clear glue ● Masking tape ● 2 paper brads ● Poster paints ● Clear gloss varnish ● Gilt disks, old brass buttons, sequins, pebbles, etc. ● Thin cord, 8 in. (20cm) long

3 When they are dry, start to cover both pieces of frame with papier-mâché. Use pieces of torn paper about 1 in. (2.5cm) wide, and when you paper around the opening in the front of the frame, try to keep the papier-mâché nice and smooth. Cover the frame pieces with three layers of papier-mâché and leave them to dry for 24 hours.

HEART-SHAPED FRAME TEMPLATE (*Thick cardboard*)

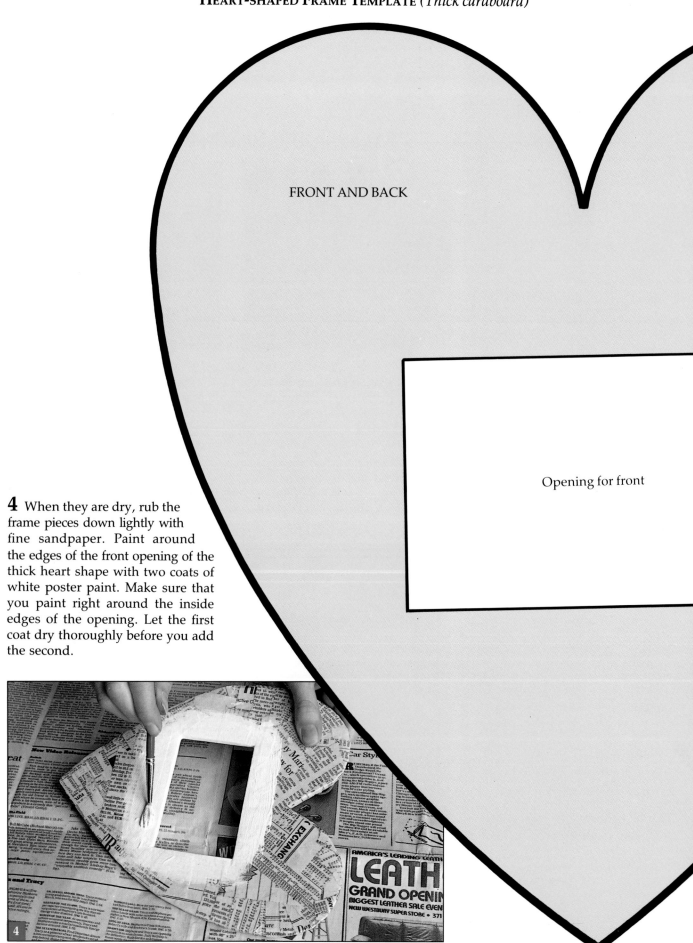

FRONT AND BACK

Opening for front

4 When they are dry, rub the frame pieces down lightly with fine sandpaper. Paint around the edges of the front opening of the thick heart shape with two coats of white poster paint. Make sure that you paint right around the inside edges of the opening. Let the first coat dry thoroughly before you add the second.

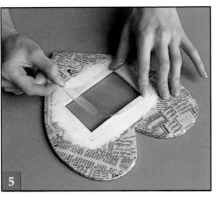

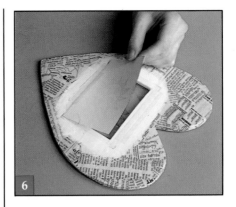

5 When the white paint is dry, lay the piece of acetate over the opening in front of the frame. It doesn't matter which side you put the acetate on, but remember that this is now the **inside** of the frame. Mark around the edges of the piece of acetate with pencil. Smear the edges with a little strong, clear glue and lay the acetate back down within your pencil marks, securing it in place with masking tape.

6 Take your picture and lay it on top of the acetate, again on the inside of the frame. Make sure that the picture is the right way around and that you can see it through the acetate from the front of the frame! When you are sure that your picture is straight and looks right from the front, tape it in place with masking tape.

7 Ask an adult to help you make two small cuts in the thin heart shape with a craft knife. Make each one 3 in. (7.5cm) from the top of the heart and 2 in. (5cm) from the center on each side. These cuts are for the paper brads, which will act as picture hangers. Push a brad into each cut. You are going to glue the thin heart to the back of the thick heart, so make sure that the heads of the brads are outside the thin heart and that their shanks are on the inside.

It is easy to check if you have put the brads in the right way around – the side with the shanks emerging from it should fit neatly over the inside of the thick heart shape. If it doesn't, remove the brads from the thin heart, and push them through from the other side. Open the brads out and tape over the flattened shanks with masking tape. Then cover the tape with a layer of papier-mâché, and leave the heart to dry overnight.

Joining the front and back

8 When the thin heart is dry, spread glue on its inside surface (a). Carefully glue the thin heart to the back of the thick heart (b) and hold the hearts together with masking tape (c).

9 Let the glue set for an hour or so, and then seal the edges of your frame with small strips of papier-mâché. Try to avoid getting splashes of glue on the acetate, especially if you are using watered-down white glue. Apply two layers of paper and leave the frame to dry for 24 hours.

10 When it is dry, rub down the frame with fine sandpaper, and paint it with two coats of white emulsion, taking special care around the heads of the brads. Allow the first coat of paint to dry thoroughly before you add the second. Let the frame dry for 2 hours.

11 Now give the frame two coats of poster paint. Leave it to dry thoroughly for 24 hours, and then paint it with 2 coats of clear gloss varnish, allowing the first coat to dry before you apply the second. Remember to clean your varnishing brush in soap and water when you have finished.

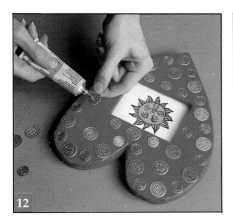

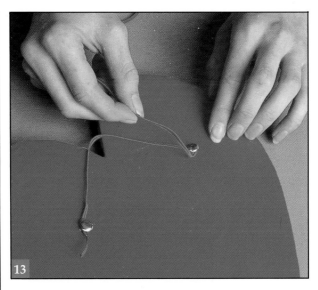

12 When the second coat of varnish is dry, take the decorations you have chosen, for example, gilt disks, and arrange them in a pattern. When you are satisfied with the design, coat the backs with strong, clear glue and press them firmly to the frame.

13 Allow the frame to dry thoroughly and tie the cord around the heads of the brads on the back. The frame is now ready to hang up.

Square Frame with Heart-shaped Opening

This frame has a distinctive heart-shaped opening. It has a hinge and is fastened at one side with a thin ribbon bow.

Although this design would be good to give as a Valentine's Day present, you could make the opening any shape you like and make the frame as large or as small as you please. You could even have several openings in the frame and keep a variety of pictures or photographs in it.

YOU WILL NEED

Thick cardboard, approximately 14 × 14 in. (36 × 36cm) ● Craft knife ● White glue ● Masking tape ● Wallpaper paste or watered down white glue ● Paper ● Fine sandpaper ● Cotton tape, 1 in. (2.5cm) wide and 8 in. (20cm) long ● Narrow cotton ribbon, 8 in. (20cm) long ● Strong, clear glue ● Poster paints ● Black India ink ● Clear gloss varnish ● Black felt, approximately 7 × 7 in. (17.5 × 17.5cm) ● Scissors

SQUARE FRAME WITH HEART-SHAPED OPENING TEMPLATE *(Thick cardbo*

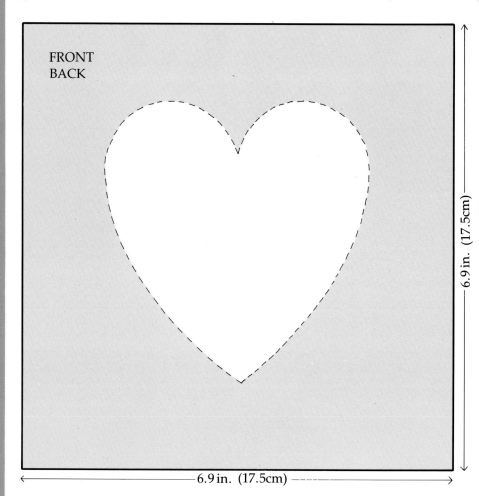

FRONT
BACK

6.9 in. (17.5cm)

6.9 in. (17.5cm)

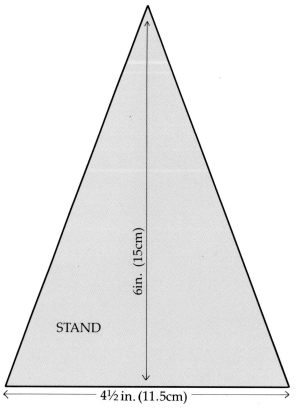

STAND

6 in. (15cm)

4½ in. (11.5cm)

Making your frame

1 Mark out the measurements for the front and back of the frame on the cardboard. Be sure to transfer the measurements correctly. Ask an adult to help you cut out the frame and stand pieces with a craft knife, because the knife will be very sharp.

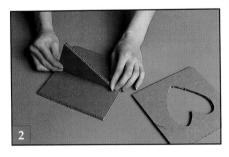

2 Measure a point halfway along the top and bottom edges of the back. Use a ruler to join these two points with a pencil line. Coat one long edge of the stand with white glue and place it along the line on the back. Hold the stand firmly in position with masking tape and leave the glue to set for a couple of hours.

3 Give the frame pieces a coat of watered-down white glue, and let them dry on a wire cake rack for 4 hours. Cover all the pieces with three layers of papier-mâché. Make sure that you do not knock the stand out of position. Let the frame pieces dry on a wire cake rack overnight.

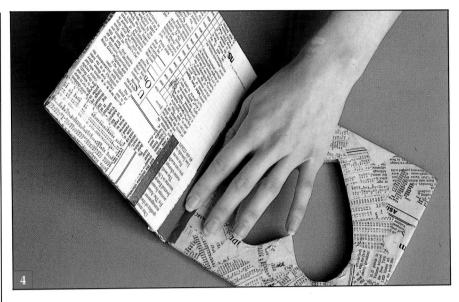

4 Lightly rub down the dry pieces with fine sandpaper. Fold the tape you are going to use as the hinge in two lengthwise and spread undiluted white glue on half of it. Glue the tape to the right-hand edge of the inside of the front of the frame. Smear glue on the other half of the tape, and stick it to the edge of the back. While the tape is drying, prop the frame slightly open so that it doesn't stick to itself.

5 When the tape is dry, open the frame. Measure two points, one halfway down the inside of the left-hand side of the front of the frame and one halfway down the right-hand side of the back. Mark these points and glue half the length of narrow ribbon to each with strong clear glue. Hold the lengths of ribbon in place with masking tape. Cover the edges of the hinge tape and the ribbon with two layers of papier-mâché. Leave the frame to dry for 24 hours.

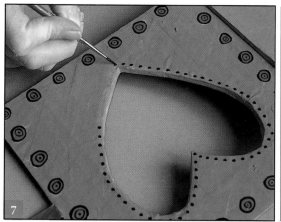

6 Lightly sand the extra papier-mâché, and give your frame two coats of white poster paint, allowing the first coat to dry before you add the second. Leave to dry.

7 Draw a design on the frame with pencil and fill it in with color. Don't forget to paint the back, too. Allow the paint to dry for 4 hours and then add detail to your design with black Indian ink. Let the frame dry overnight and then apply two coats of clear gloss varnish.

8 Take the piece of black felt and use scissors to cut it to the same size as the back. Smear it with undiluted PVA adhesive, and stick it carefully to the back so that it covers the edge of the thin ribbon. Let your frame dry overnight before you use it.

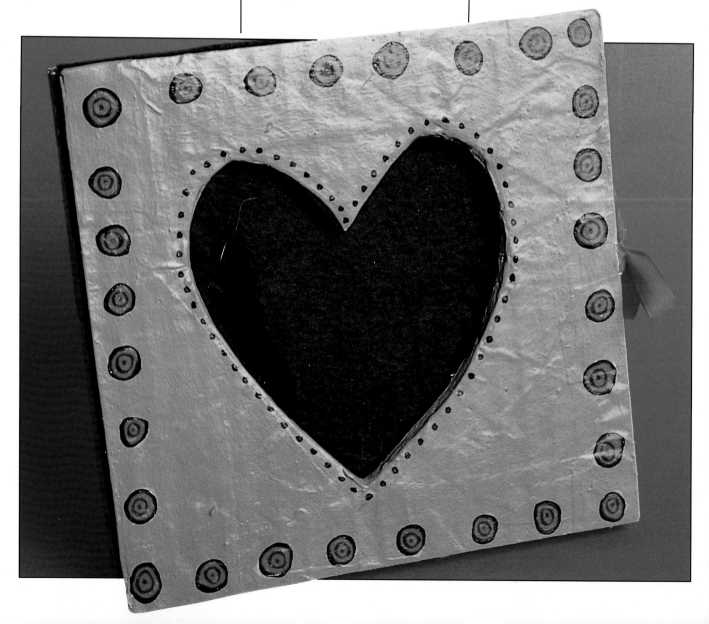

FESTIVALS

This section contains some projects that you can make in papier-mâché to celebrate the year's special occasions. The Christmas decorations are jolly and bright, and they can be made in several sizes. You could make a robin several times the size of the template, for example, and hang it from ribbon as a decorative plaque. Other shapes would make good wall decorations, too – bells and holly leaves, for example. Rather than painting the tree decorations, you might like to cover the shapes in gold, silver, or colored foil and add a touch of sparkle to your tree!

Easter bunnies and Easter eggs can be made over molded clay, which is removed when the paper has dried. You could leave an opening under the bunny and fill him with candy for an extra surprise, as is done in several countries. It would be fun to use the same method to make an Easter chicken to accompany him.

Easter eggs can be made in several sizes, and if you plan to make a lot, you could even buy special metal egg molds – which are really for making chocolate eggs – and use them for your papier-mâché if you don't want to make them from clay. If you do use a metal mold, remember to grease it with petroleum jelly first.

Christmas Cutouts

These cheerful cutouts can be used as decorations to brighten up your Christmas tree, but you needn't stop there – they will lend a festive atmosphere to any part of the house and will look especially decorative displayed at a window.

Once you've painted and varnished them, you might like to add sequins or fake gemstones to give them an extra sparkle!

YOU WILL NEED

Tracing paper • Thin cardboard, approximately 10 × 10½ in. (25 × 26cm) for each decoration • Scissors • Wallpaper paste or watered-down white glue • Paper • Fine sandpaper • Poster paints • Black India ink • Clear gloss varnish • Darning needle • White glue (undiluted) • Metal screw eyes, one for each decoration • Thin colored cord, 8 in. (20 cm) for each decoration

CHRISTMAS DECORATIONS TEMPLATES *(Thin cardboard)*

BOW

STAR

ROBIN

Making the cutouts

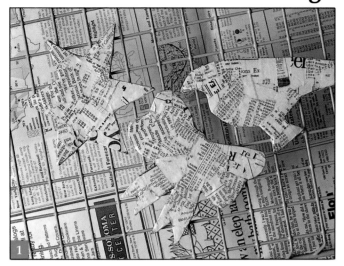

1 Trace the decoration shapes from the book and transfer them to your thin cardboard. Cut out the cardboard shapes with scissors. Give each decoration a coat of watered-down white glue and let them dry on a wire cake rack for about 4 hours. When they have dried somewhat, cover your pieces with pasted paper, using strips about ½ in. (12mm) wide and 2 in. (5cm) long.

2 Cover each decoration with three layers of papier-mâché and place them on a wire cake rack to dry for 24 hours.

3 When the shapes are dry, smooth them lightly with fine sandpaper and give them two layers of white poster paint; allow the first coat to dry properly before you add the second. Let the paint dry for 4 hours.

4 Draw in the features or patterns on your decorations with pencil and start to apply the colour with your paints. You will probably have to use two coats of paint to cover the white paint properly.

5 Leave the paint to dry for 4 hours, then use black India ink to outline and emphasize the details. Let the decorations dry overnight.

7 When the varnish is dry, ask an adult to help you to make a hole in the top of each decoration with a darning needle. Dab a little white glue into each hole, and screw the metal eyes into each hole as far as they will go. Be careful to keep the screws straight so that they do not emerge from the sides of your decorations. Leave the decorations to dry for a few hours until the glue has set. All that remains to do is to tie the thin cord to the top of each metal eye. Tie a loop in the top of each length of cord once it is fastened to a decoration and hang it from your tree.

6 When they are thoroughly dry, paint your decorations with two coats of clear gloss varnish, allowing the first coat to dry properly before you add the second. Remember, as always, to clean your brush in soap and water when you have finished with it.

Easter Eggs

These Easter eggs are made in the same way as the bunny, using modeling clay as a mold. A piece of thin cardboard is used to make a lip to hold the two halves together.

If you are giving the eggs as Easter gifts, you might like to put little presents – charms or candy, for example – inside them as a surprise.

Making the Easter eggs

1 Break the clay into lumps that are about the size you want each finished egg to be. Roll each piece of clay between the palms of your hands to soften it, and then work it into an egg shape. Add or take away clay as necessary, and finally cover the eggs with petroleum jelly.

2 When you are satisfied with your egg shapes, tear up your paper into pieces about the size of postage stamps and start to cover the eggs. Try to mold the paper smoothly over the clay. Cover each egg shape with eight layers of papier-mâché, and leave them to dry in a warm place for 2–3 days.

3 When the papier-mâché feels dry, ask an adult to cut each egg into two equal halves. It is probably easiest to make the first cut with a craft knife through the papier-mâché to the clay all the way around each egg, and then to use a kitchen knife with a serrated blade – a bread knife, for example – to saw through the clay.

YOU WILL NEED

Modeling clay, 4–8 oz. (150–250g) for small to medium eggs; 1 lb. (500g) for large eggs ● Petroleum jelly ● Paper ● Wallpaper paste or watered-down white glue ● Craft knife ● Serrated knife ● Palette-knife ● Fine sandpaper ● Poster paints ● Black India ink ● Clear gloss varnish ● Pieces of thin white cardboard ● Clear, strong glue

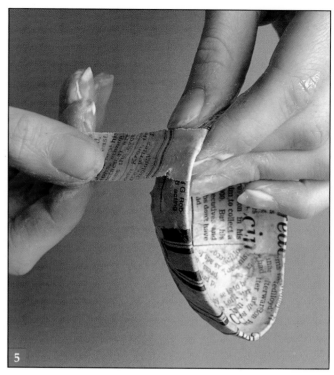

5 Bind all around the cut edges of each empty shell with small strips of paper, approximately ½ × 2 in. (12mm × 5cm). One layer of binding strips will be sufficient. Let the shells dry overnight on a wire cake rack.

4 Leave the opened eggs to dry on a wire cake rack for an hour or so, and then, using the blade of a thin palette-knife, gently prize the clay away from the walls of each papier-mâché egg.

6 Lightly sand the shells inside and out, and give each one two coats of white poster paint, allowing the first coat to dry thoroughly before you add the second.

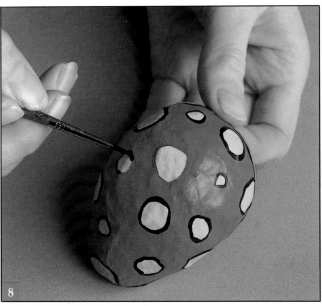

7 Draw designs on the outside of the painted shells and start to fill them in with color. You will probably need two coats of paint to achieve a good, deep color.

8 Allow the paint to dry for 4 hours, and outline your designs with black India ink. Let the eggs dry overnight.

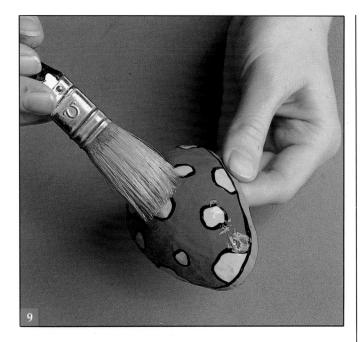

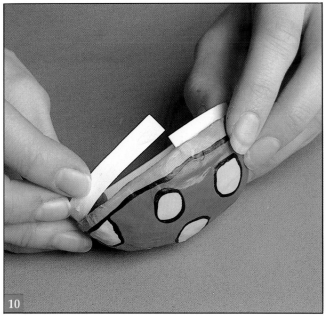

9 Give each eggshell two coats of clear gloss varnish. Paint the varnish on one side at a time, and let it dry completely before you do the other. Allow the first coat to dry on each side of your eggs before you add the second.

10 Measure around the inside edge of one half of each egg. Cut a piece of thin white cardboard this length and about ½ in. (12mm) wide. Coat the card with clear, strong glue down one long edge, and spread a thin line of the same glue around the inside edge of one eggshell. Let the glue on both surfaces dry slightly and press the card around the inside of the eggshell. Make sure the ends join neatly.

11 Let your eggs dry thoroughly before you fit them together.

Easter Bunny

This Easter bunny was made on molded clay, cut in half and then joined back together with small strips of paper. Before it was joined together, it was painted white inside because it is open at the bottom so that candy can be stuffed inside it. In some countries, candy is sealed inside papier-mâché toys, which are smashed open by the children who receive them. But it would be a shame to break this bunny after you've decorated him!

YOU WILL NEED

Modeling clay, 1 lb. (500g) ●
Pottery modeling tools or similar
● Paper ● Petroleum jelly ●
Wallpaper paste or watered-
down white glue ● Craft knife ●
Serrated knife ● Palette-knife ●
Masking tape ● Scissors ● White
glue (undiluted) ● Fine
sandpaper ● Poster paints ●
Black India ink ● Clear gloss
varnish

Making your bunny

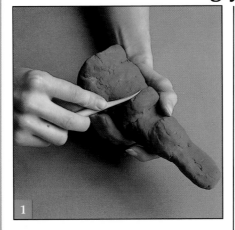

1 Soften the clay between the palms of your hands and shape it into a block about 8 in. (20cm) long, 3 in. (7.5cm) deep and 3 in. (7.5cm) wide. Use pottery modeling tools or something similar to mold the bunny shape. The bunny illustrated has a very simple design, but you could make it more ornate if you wanted to.

2 Smear a little petroleum jelly over the clay, thinly and evenly.

3 When you are happy with the shape of your clay bunny, tear up the paper into pieces the size of postage stamps and start to cover him. Take care to mold the paper smoothly, and try to make sure that each layer covers the bunny completely before you begin to apply the next, so that he doesn't have any thin patches. It is a good idea to use two colors of paper if you can so that you can alternate the colors with each layer. Cover the bunny with eight layers of papier-mâché, and put him in a warm place to dry for 2–3 days.

4 When the papier-mâché feels dry, draw a line down the center of the front and back of your bunny, making sure that it divides him into two equal halves. Ask an adult to cut the bunny in half for you by making an initial cut with a craft knife and then slicing through him with a serrated knife such as a bread knife.

5 Place the opened halves of the bunny on a wire cake rack. Let the edges harden for an hour or so, and then use the blade of a thin palette-knife to push the clay gently away from the edges of the paper casts. Lever the clay out of each half, and leave the papier-mâché to dry overnight on a wire cake rack.

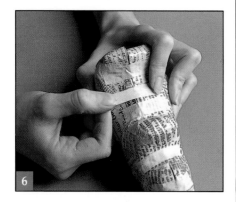

6 Tape the two halves of your bunny together, making sure that they join accurately, and draw an oval on the underside.

7 Untape the halves and cut out the oval with a pair of scissors. Pick any small traces of clay off the inside of each cast, and paint the insides with two coats of white poster paint, allowing the first to dry completely before you add the second.

8 When the painted insides are dry, smear the cut edges of each half bunny with undiluted white glue. Join the two halves together, making sure that they fit closely, and anchor them firmly with masking tape. Allow the bunny to dry on a wire cake rack for 2 hours. Cover the join with two layers of small paper strips, and bind the edges of the oval in the underside of the bunny. Let him dry overnight on a wire cake rack.

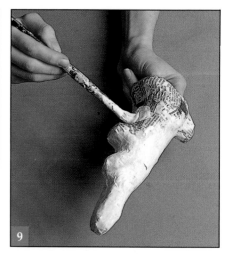

9 Lightly sand down the surface of your bunny with fine sandpaper, and give him two coats of white paint, allowing the first to dry before you add the second. Remember to paint over the paper strips on the inside edge of the oval opening.

Decorating your bunny

10 When the white paint has dried, draw the design on your bunny with pencil and start to fill it in with color. You will probably need to use two coats to achieve a good, deep color. Let the paint dry for 4 hours, and then define the design with black India ink. Let the bunny dry overnight.

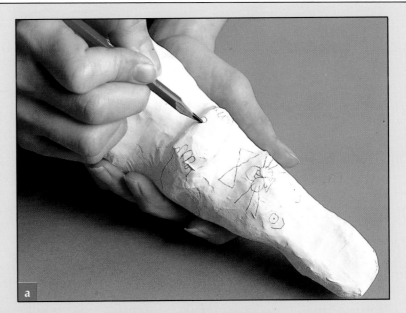

a

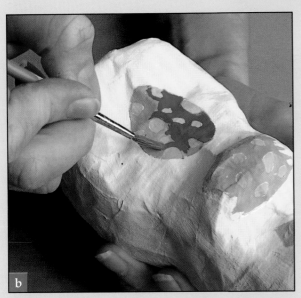

b

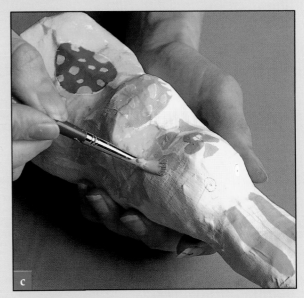

c

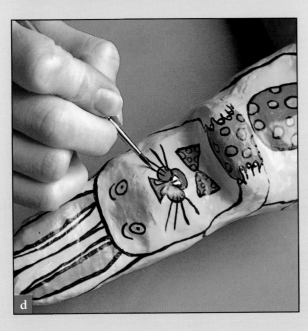

d

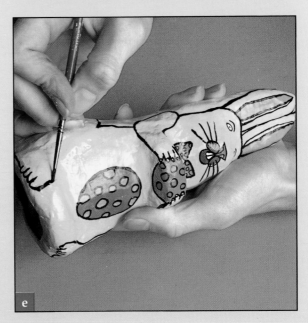

e

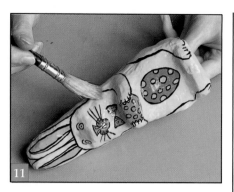

11 Give your bunny two coats of clear gloss varnish, allowing the first to dry thoroughly before you add the second. Remember to clean your brushes in soap and water when you have finished. When your bunny is dry, you can fill him with candy.

HELPFUL HINT...

If you make a mistake when you are adding details in black India ink, let the ink dry and then paint over it with a little white paint paint. When the paint is dry, you can easily cover up the mistake with the original background colour and draw in the black line again.

TOYS

Papier-mâché is ideal for making toys because it is so versatile – you can make almost anything you like with a little thought and planning! This section shows you how to make masks, a mobile, a jointed toy elephant, and puppets. You can let your imagination run wild to create fabulous masks and puppets. You could make characters from your favorite books and games or perform a masked play with your friends. Put on a puppet show at your school or club – you could ask your friends to write short plays and sketches and perform them with puppets.

Dolls are also fun to make in papier-mâché. You can make them over molded clay, in the same way as the Easter bunny in the Festivals section. Make them rigid, all in one piece so that they cannot be repositioned, or make the arms and legs separately and join the limbs to the body with round elastic.

Jointed Elephant

This handsome elephant has movable legs, ears, and tail. His body is made from thick cardboard, while thinner cardboard is used for his limbs, ears, and tail, which are held in place with paper brads. These brads, which can be bought from stationery shops, act as pivots and allow you to reposition the elephant's limbs.

JOINTED ELEPHANT TEMPLATES *(Thick and thin cardboard)*

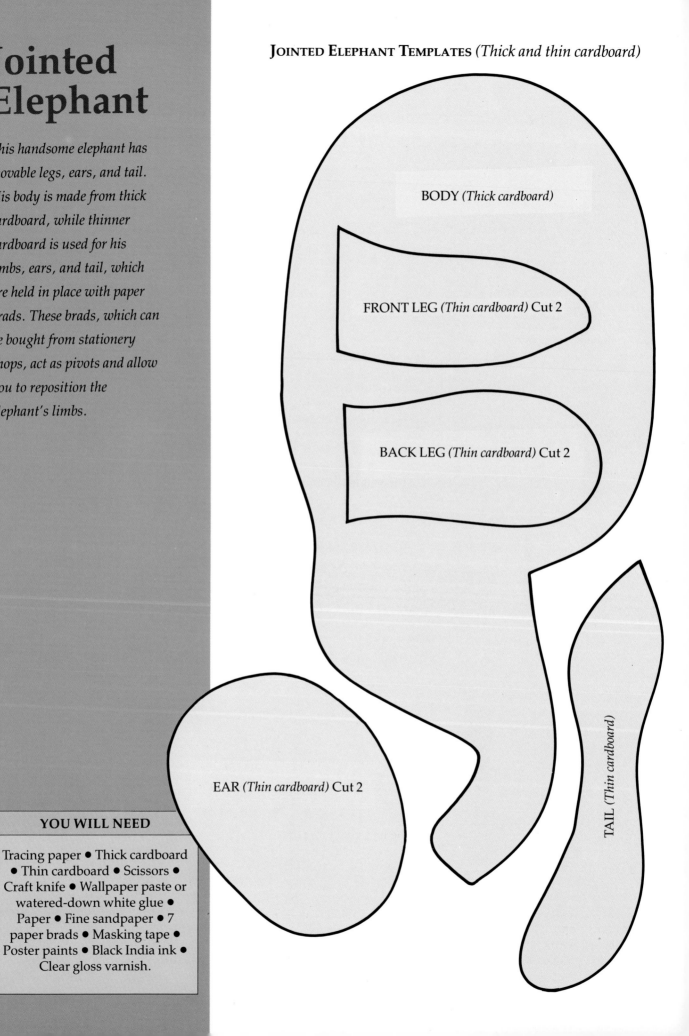

BODY *(Thick cardboard)*

FRONT LEG *(Thin cardboard)* Cut 2

BACK LEG *(Thin cardboard)* Cut 2

EAR *(Thin cardboard)* Cut 2

TAIL *(Thin cardboard)*

Making your elephant

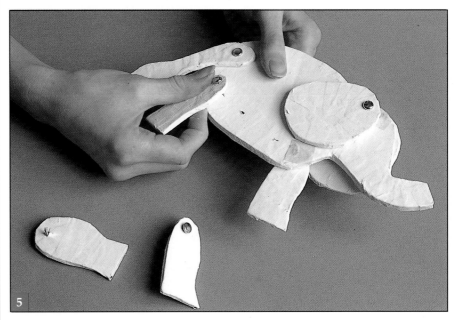

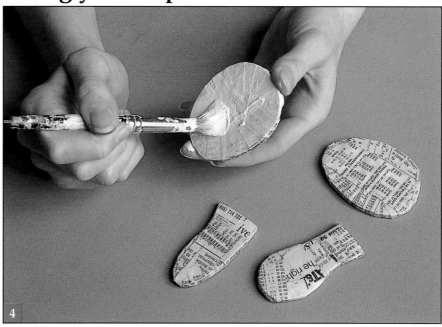

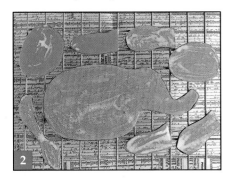

1 Trace the elephant pieces from the pattern and transfer them to the cardboard. Remember to use thick cardboard for the body and thinner card for the movable parts. Cut around each piece with scissors. Ask an adult to help you cut the thicker cardboard, as the craft knife will be very sharp.

2 When all the pieces are cut, give them a coat of watered-down white glue to help prevent them from warping when papier-mâché is added. Leave the pieces to dry on a wire cake rack for 4 hours.

3 Tear your paper into thin, short strips, ½ in. (12mm) wide and 3 in. (7.5cm) long, and cover the pieces of cardboard with three coats of papier-mâché. Leave the shapes to dry overnight on a wire cake rack.

4 When the shapes are dry, smooth them with fine sandpaper and give each one two coats of white poster paint, taking care to let the paint dry thoroughly between each coat.

5 The legs, ears, and tail are joined to the body with brads. So that the shanks of each brad can pass through the cardboard, you have to make a small incision toward the top center of each movable piece. Ask an adult to help you with this, because you need a craft knife, which will have a very sharp blade. Pass the shanks of a brad through each little hole. Ask an adult to help you make similar incisions in the elephant's body for the brads to pass through. You need to make seven holes, one for each of the legs and ears and one for the tail. Remember that some pins have to go from the front to the back of the body and some from the back to the front, but you can make room for them by moving each piece to one side once it has been fixed.

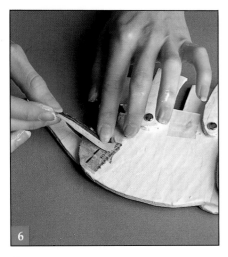

6 When all the brads are in place, cover the opened-out shanks of each one with masking tape. Cover the tape with strips of papier-mâché, and leave your elephant to dry overnight, propped upright if possible.

7 When the papier-mâché is dry, carefully sand it down and give the elephant two coats of white paint, allowing the first to dry completely before you add the second.

Painting your elephant

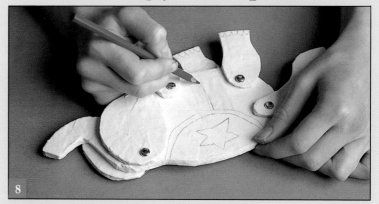

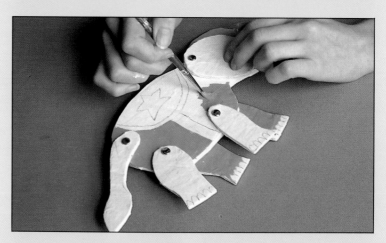

HELPFUL HINT . . .

Leave your papier-mâché objects in the driest place in the house – but away from direct heat.

8 Draw in the elephant's toenails, tusks, eye, and blanket, and paint the elephant with poster paints. You will have to move his limbs carefully so that you can paint him properly, and you will probably have to come back to the underside of his ears and legs several times because you won't be able to paint everything all at once. Remember that your elephant has two sides, so paint both sides the same.

9 When you have finished painting the colors in, let your elephant dry for 4 hours, and then add the outlines and details in black India ink. Leave your elephant to dry overnight, and then give him two coats of clear gloss varnish, allowing the first coat to dry thoroughly before you add the second. When you are varnishing around his limbs, take care that they don't stick to his body. When you have finished varnishing, clean your brush thoroughly with soap and water.

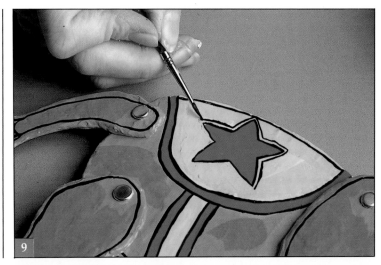

Face Mask

One of the simplest ways of making a mask is to use a balloon as a mold. The resulting paper shape, when cut in half lengthwise, will make a lovely oval, which can be painted just as it is or used as a base on which to build facial features with cardboard, chicken wire, and so on.

The mask illustrated here is decorated very simply with eyebrows, a pair of glasses, and a nose cut from cardboard and stuck on. Ears are added, and fake fur is used to create sideburns and bushy eyebrows.

YOU WILL NEED

Tape measure • 1 balloon • Petroleum jelly • Paper • Wallpaper paste or watered-down white glue • String • Scissors • Small pieces of thin cardboard • Strong, clear glue • Masking tape • Fine sandpaper • Poster paints • Black India ink • Clear gloss varnish • Fake fur, cotton balls, string, yarn, pieces of felt and similar for hair, beard, and moustache • Darning needle • Round elastic • Tracing paper

1 Measure your face from about 1 in. (2.5cm) above the start of your hairline to 1 in. (2.5cm) below the end of your chin. Blow up the balloon – you may have to ask an adult to help you – until it is slightly longer than your hairline-to-chin measurement. Tie the end of the balloon tightly to stop it from going down, and grease it with a thin layer of petroleum jelly. This will allow the dried paper cast to be removed from the balloon and will also mean that if the balloon does go down slightly, your papier-mâché won't shrivel with it! Place the balloon in an empty bowl.

2 Tear up your paper into strips about 1 in. (2.5cm) wide and 10 in. (25cm) long and start to cover the balloon.

3 You will find it easier to remember whether you have finished a layer or not if you use two different colors of paper, alternating colors with each layer. When you have covered your balloon with eight layers of papier-mâché, tie a length of string to the end and suspend it in a warm place to dry. It will probably take 3 days to dry out completely.

4 When the papier-mâché feels dry, burst the balloon by sticking a pin through the paper; pull the deflated balloon out of the cast by the string. Draw a line lengthwise around the center of the papier-mâché. Ask an adult to help you cut around the line with sharp scissors.

5 Take one of the paper halves. This will be your mask. You will need to mark the openings for your mouth and eyes on the inside of the mask. The easiest way to do this is to put some lipstick on your mouth, fit the balloon half over your face and, when it feels comfortably in place, "kiss" the inside. The lipstick will leave a clear mark that you can use as a guide for the mouth hole, which can be cut into any shape you want.

7 Now position the glasses, nose, and eyebrow pieces on your mask. Anchor them in place with strong, clear glue, and secure them firmly with masking-tape while they dry.

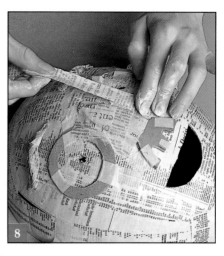

8 When the glue is dry, cover the cardboard additions with two layers of papier-mâché. Bind the cut edges of the mouth hole, and, if you have made them large, the edges of the eye holes. Also bind the outside edge of the mask, and leave it to dry for 24 hours.

6 To find out where the eye holes should go, measure a straight line from the top of your lower lip to the top of your nose, between your eyes. Mark this on the inside of your mask, taking the lipstick mark as your starting point. Now measure from the top of your nose to the center of each eye. Mark these measurements on the inside of your mask. Make a small hole at each center eye mark, and if you have measured correctly, you will be able to see through. Make the eye holes as big or small as you want, but **do not** try to enlarge the holes while you are holding the mask against your face.

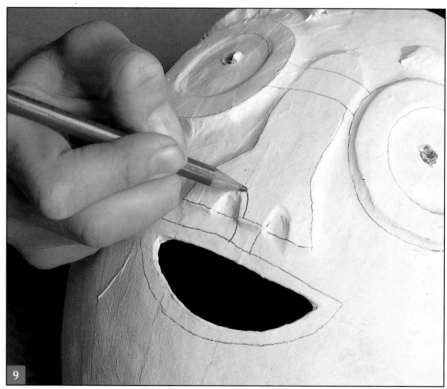

9 Smooth the surface of the dry mask with fine sandpaper and give it two coats of white paint, both inside and out, allowing the first coat to dry before you add the second. When the paint is dry, draw the design onto the mask.

Painting the mask

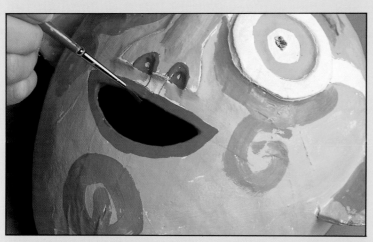

10 Draw a design on the mask in pencil, and start to fill it in with color. You can make your decoration lifelike, or you could let your imagination run riot and create a strange and fabulous face.

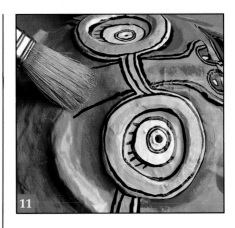

11 Leave the paint to dry for 4 hours. Outline your design with black India ink and let the mask dry overnight. Paint the mask with two coats of clear gloss varnish, allowing the first coat to dry properly before you add the second. Remember to clean your varnishing brush in soap and water when you have finished.

12 When the varnish is dry, you can stick on hair and beards and moustaches. Lots of materials can be used for this, including fake fur, cotton, string, yarn and felt. Use strong, clear glue; then leave your mask to dry overnight. All that remains to do is to attach the elastic to your mask so that you can wear it. Place the mask against your face, and ask a friend to mark a spot just above your ear on each side of the mask.

13 Ask an adult to help you make a hole at each spot with a darning needle. Enlarge the holes until they are wide enough for the elastic to pass through. Thread the elastic through the mask from the inside to the outside and tie a knot in the end. Push the elastic through the other hole from the outside to the inside, pull it tight and tie a knot. Cut off the excess elastic; your mask is now ready to wear.

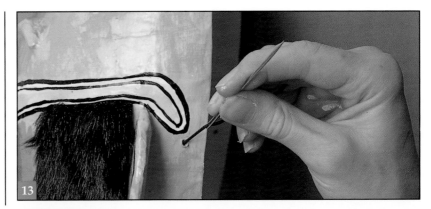

Monster Mask

This monster mask is made, like the other mask, over a balloon mold, but the resulting paper shape is cut around rather than lengthwise, so that it fits over the head like a helmet. The monster has strange, golden protruberances growing from the top of its head and seven eyes, but the effect is humorous rather than scary. The golden spikes have been made with empty cones from rolls of yarn, but if you can't find these, you can make your own cones from rolled-up cardboard just as easily.

YOU WILL NEED

Tape measure • 1 balloon •
Petroleum jelly • Paper •
Wallpaper paste or watered-down white glue • String •
Scissors • Craft knife • White glue (undiluted) • 6 empty knitting wool cones or cones made of thin cardboard •
Masking tape • Fine sandpaper •
Poster paints • Black India ink •
Nontoxic gold craft paint • Clear gloss varnish

Making a monster mask

1 Measure around your head, holding the tape measure over the mid-point of your ears. Blow up the balloon – you may need an adult to help you at this point – until it is slightly larger at its widest point than your head measurement. Tie the balloon tightly, and grease it with a thin coat of petroleum jelly. Stand the balloon in an empty bowl.

2 Tear the paper into strips about 1 in. (2.5cm) wide and 10 in. (25cm) long and cover the balloon with eight layers of papier-mâché. If possible, use two colors of paper alternately so that you can see when you have finished each layer. Tie a length of string to the end, and hang your balloon to dry in a warm place for 2–3 days.

3 When the papier-mâché is dry, burst the balloon by sticking a pin through it; pull the deflated balloon through the bottom of the cast. Measure a line from the center of the top of your head down the front of your face to the bridge of your nose. This line should be long enough to reach to about 1 in. (2.5cm) below your eyes. Transfer this measurement to the front of your balloon. Make a pencil mark at the center of the balloon, measure straight down until you have the same length as the distance from the top of your head to your nose and make a mark. Repeat this measurement from the same central point several times, working your way around the balloon until you have a row of dots. Join this line of dots and ask an adult to help you cut along it with sharp scissors.

4 Place the paper "helmet" over your head, and hold the paper between finger and thumb, fingers outside and thumbs directly in front of each eye – your fingers will show you where. Ask someone to help you mark the spots on the outside of the mask. Draw in two eye shapes, and ask an adult to help you cut out these shapes with a craft knife. **Never** try to make the eye holes while you are wearing the mask. Arrange the cones, about 4 in. (10cm) high, on the crown of your mask. When you are happy with their position, draw around the base of each. Coat the underside of each cone with white glue, and place them back in position inside the drawn lines. Hold them firmly in position with masking tape. Let the glue set for a couple of hours, then cover the cones with two layers of papier-mâché. Make sure that you cover the joins well.

5 Bind around the cutout eyes and around the edge of the mask with small pieces of papier-mâché. Stand it on a wire cake rack to dry for 24 hours. When the mask is dry, sand it lightly with fine sandpaper and give it two coats of white paint, allowing the first coat to dry thoroughly before you add the second.

Painting the mask

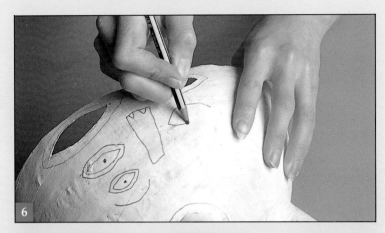

6 When the paint has dried, draw a design on the mask and start to fill it in with color. The mask illustrated here has been decorated very simply, but it would lend itself perfectly to more flamboyant designs. When you have finished painting your mask, let it dry for 4 hours and then outline your design with black India ink. Paint the spikes with gold craft paint, and leave the mask to dry for 24 hours.

7 The mask should now be painted with two coats of clear gloss varnish, but be careful not to varnish over the gold paint on the spikes. Let the first coat of varnish dry before adding the second coat, and remember to clean your brushes in warm soapy water when you have finished.

Mobile

The fish in this mobile float gracefully around a central shell, suspended from a crossbar. Mobiles have long been favorites with children and babies, and are often hung over their cribs and beds to amuse them. Your mobile need not feature fish – brightly colored geometric shapes would be very effective – and, of course, you'll probably want to be more adventurous than this. The main thing to remember when you choose your shapes is that they will have to hang in the same mobile and should look as if they belong together!

YOU WILL NEED

Tracing paper ● Thin cardboard, approximately 10 × 10 in. (25 × 25cm) ● Thick cardboard, approximately 10 × 10 in. (25 × 25cm) ● Scissors or craft knife ● Wallpaper paste or watered-down white glue ● Paper ● White glue (undiluted) ● Masking tape ● Fine sandpaper ● Poster paints ● Black India ink ● Clear gloss varnish ● 6 metal screw eyes ● Darning needle ● Thin cord or strong thread, approximately 45 in. (112cm)

MOBILE TEMPLATES *(Thick and thin cardboard)*

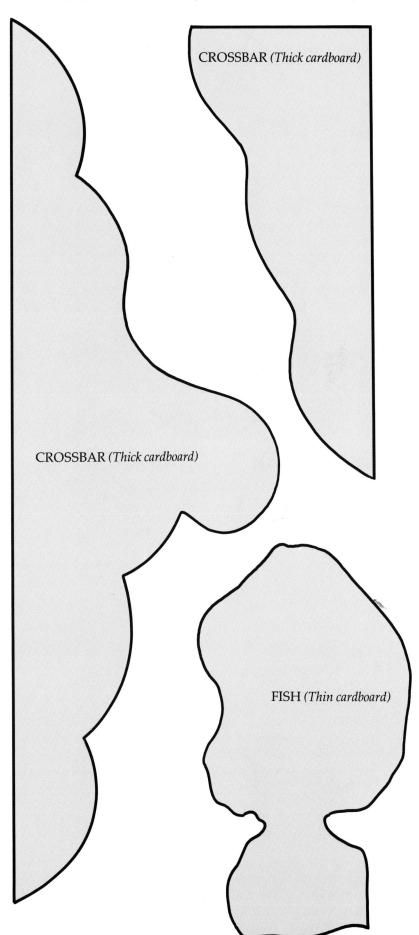

CROSSBAR *(Thick cardboard)*

CROSSBAR *(Thick cardboard)*

FISH *(Thin cardboard)*

FISH *(Thin cardboard)*

FISH *(Thin cardboard)*

SHELL *(Thin cardboard)*

SHELL *(Thin cardboard)*

As mobiles are suspended in the air, you might like to make one that features flying things – planes, insects, or hot air balloons, for example – or things that appear in the sky, such as stars or planets. Perhaps these are flying fish in the mobile illustrated here!

Making the mobile

1 Trace the fish and shell motifs from the book, and transfer the shapes to the thin cardboard. Trace the crossbar shapes, and transfer them to the thick cardboard. Cut out the shapes using scissors or a craft knife, but ask an adult to help you if you use a craft knife because the blade will be very sharp. Coat each cutout piece with watered-down white glue, and leave them to dry on a wire cake rack for 4 hours.

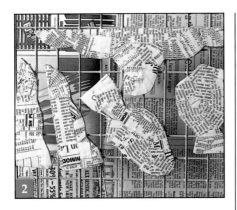

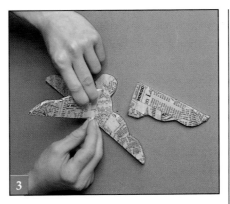

2 Tear your paper into strips about ½ in. (12mm) wide and 3 in. (7.5cm) long and start to cover your cardboard shapes. Three layers of papier-mâché will be sufficient for each fish. Try to keep the edges neat and smooth, as the finished effect will be more pleasing. Cover the shell motif and sections of crossbar in the same way and leave your papered shapes to dry on a wire cake rack for 24 hours.

3 Take the dry cross-pieces and join them at right angles as shown in the photograph. Coat the edges of both short pieces with undiluted white glue, and, after positioning them on the main piece of the crossbar, anchor them firmly with masking tape. When the glue has set for a couple of hours, paper over the joints with thin strips of papier-mâché. Let the crossbar dry for 24 hours.

4 When all the pieces are dry, rub them down lightly with fine sandpaper and give each piece two coats of white poster paint; remember to allow the first coat to dry before you add the second one.

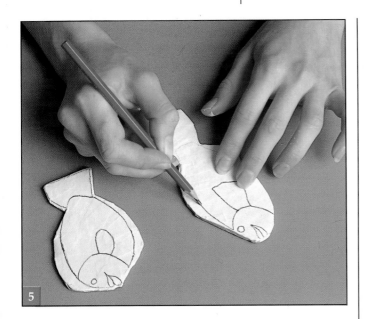

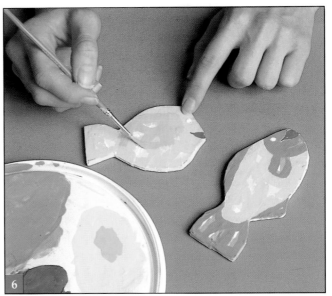

5 Draw the features on the white fish shapes with pencil. Try to give each fish a different expression so that your mobile looks interesting. Draw the spiral on the shell shape, and don't forget the shell on the top of the crossbar!

6 Paint the mobile pieces. If you want to create a mottled effect, paint your pieces with progressively darker shades of the same color, allowing each coat of paint to dry thoroughly before adding the next one.

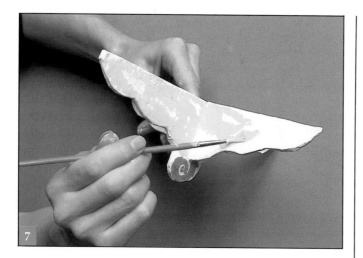

7 The crossbar is decorated simply in varying shades of yellow and orange. As with the fish and shell, a light color is used for the first coat of paint, and this is followed by two or three slightly darker shades, finishing with orange. Let the paint dry, and then add the black outlines in India ink.

8 Varnish the finished pieces of mobile before you join them together. Give each piece two coats of varnish, allowing plenty of drying time between each coat. Remember to clean your varnishing brush with soap and water when you have finished.

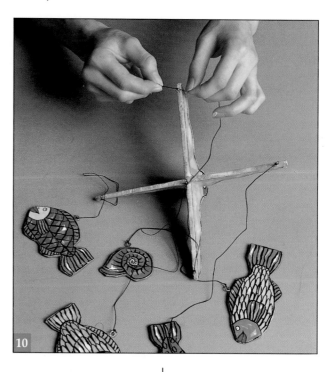

9 The fish and the shell are suspended from the crossbar by thin cord or strong thread, which is fastened to a metal eye screwed into the center of each piece. To attach the metal eye, use a darning needle to make a hole in the back of each fish, halfway along its length. Make a hole in the same way in the top of the shell. Dab a little undiluted white glue into each hole, and carefully screw a metal hook into each piece. Don't turn the screw too roughly or it may go in crooked and emerge from the side of your fish!

10 Make holes about ½ in. (12mm) from the end of each arm of the crossbar. Dab them with glue and screw in the metal eyes carefully. Attach an eye in the center of the crossbar from which the shell will be suspended. Make sure that you place it squarely, so that the shell looks balanced. Finally, screw an eye into the top of the crossbar, in the center back of the shell. The fish and shell are now ready to be sus-

pended from the crossbar. A mobile looks best if its decorations are hung at varying heights, so that it is possible to see each piece clearly. With this in mind, cut four pieces of cord or thread of different lengths. Tie the end of each thread to the metal eyes in the back of each fish. Use a double knot to make sure that the thread is firmly held. Tie the other end of each piece of thread to a different arm of the crossbar.

11 Your mobile is now ready to hang up. Decide how far you want it to drop from the ceiling or from wherever it is going to hang, and cut an appropriate length of thread. If you are making this mobile for a very young child or baby, make sure that it is hung high enough to be out of their reach so that they can't pull it down and chew it! Tie one end of the thread to the eye in the top of the crossbar, and make a loop in the other end. The mobile can now be hung in place. It will look very effective if it is hung where there is a slight breeze to move it, and you may even like to tie bells to the threads so that it tinkles as it moves!

HELPFUL HINT . . .

When you have finished varnishing, always clean your brush carefully in soapy water. If you use the sort of varnish that requires turpentine to clean your brushes, ask an adult to help you.

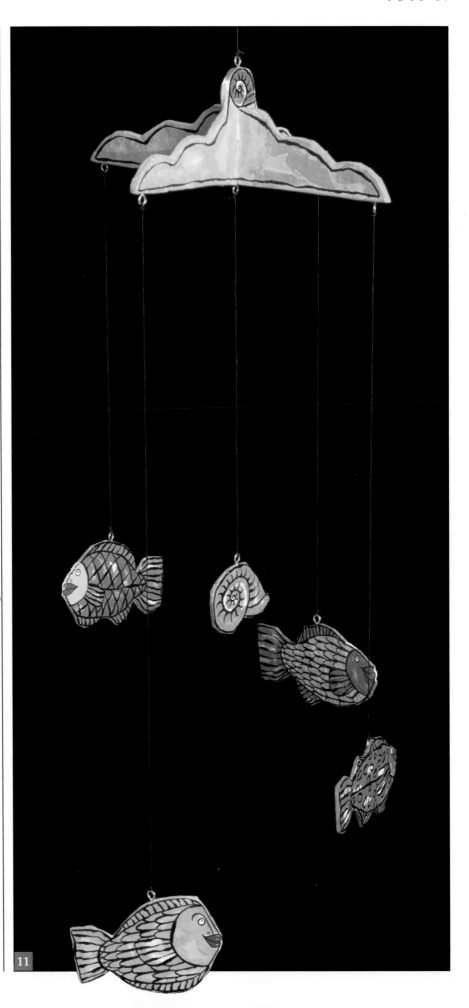

11

Puppets

Puppets are great fun, and there are several ways of making them. Here is one of the simplest and most effective methods.

This sort of puppet is known as a glove puppet because it fits over your hand like a glove. You use your middle finger to hold its head upright and your other fingers to operate its hands.

Each puppet's head is modeled in clay, which is removed when the papier-mâché has dried and been cut open. The two halves of the head are then glued back together again. Features can be added in paper pulp after the clay is removed.

YOU WILL NEED

Modeling clay, about 1 lb. (500g) for each puppet head ● Pottery modeling tools or similar ● Paper ● Wallpaper paste or watered-down white glue ● Craft knife ● Serrated knife ● Palette-knife ● White glue (undiluted) ● Masking tape ● Fine sandpaper ● Poster paints ● Black India ink ● Clear gloss varnish ● Felt, 2 pieces approximately 9 × 9 in. (23 × 23cm) for each puppet, and scraps for hands ● Tracing paper ● Plastic-headed pins ● Needle and thread ● Decorative braid, approximately 28 in. (70cm) for each puppet ● Strong, clear glue

TUNIC FOR PUPPETS TEMPLATES

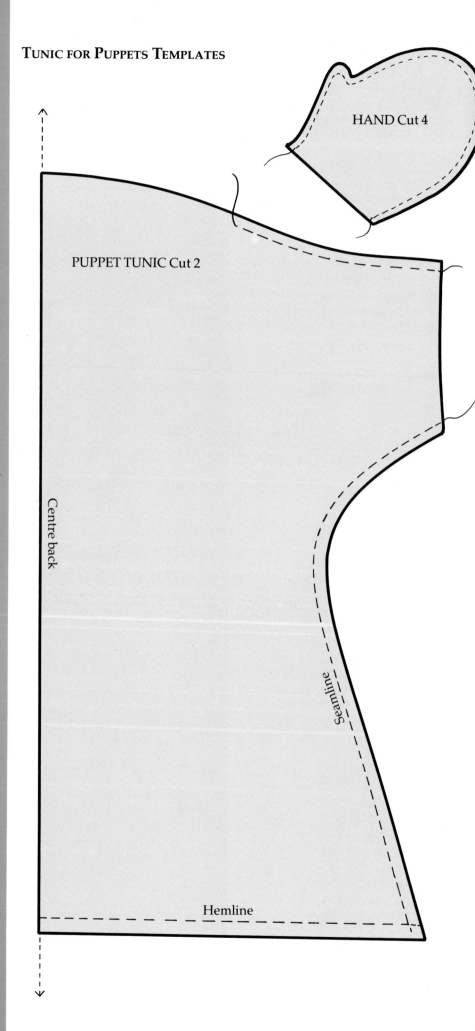

HAND Cut 4

PUPPET TUNIC Cut 2

Centre back

Seamline

Hemline

Your puppet's face should be painted in a striking way. If the character it portrays is usually happy, paint it with a beaming, jolly face. If it is a king or queen, try to make it look regal and haughty. Remember, the puppet may be 10 ft. (3m) or more away from your audience, if you use it in a puppet theater and the puppet performs inside it, so it is important that its features are bold and bright.

The puppets featured here are wearing dresses made from brightly colored felt with sparkly gold braid trims. However, it would be easy to make really ornate costumes for them, using sumptuous fabrics, sequins, fake fur, and so on. The costumes can be sewn by hand or machine, so don't despair if you haven't got a sewing machine!

Making the puppets

1 Form your clay into a large lump about 4 in. (10cm) high and 3 in. (7.5cm) thick. When you are satisfied with the size of the lump, start modeling your puppet's features. You should aim to make the mold as accurate as you can, with the eyes, nose, and mouth where you want them. At this stage, however, there is no need to make the details too fine, because they will be lost when the clay is covered with paper. Remember that you can accentuate features with paper pulp when the clay has been removed.

2 Use small pieces of paper about the size of postage stamps, because you will be able to mold the papier-mâché more closely and smoothly around the clay. When you have covered the clay with eight layers of papier-mâché, lay the head on a wire tray to dry. It may take 3–4 days to dry completely, but if you leave it in a warm place, it should be ready to cut open after 48 hours. When the head feels dry on the outside, it should be cut open and the clay removed. Ask an adult to do the cutting for you, as it will be necessary to use a craft knife to make the first cut. Cut all the way around the head, making sure that the cutting line is straight. It doesn't matter whether the head is divided down the nose or through the ears, as long as the line is straight. When the initial cut has been made, it is a good idea to finish the cutting with a serrated knife – a bread knife, for example – as it will be awkward to cut through the depth of clay with a short-bladed knife.

3 Once the head is cut in two, let the inside edges of the paper casts dry for 1–2 hours; otherwise, they might be a bit too fragile to remove the clay. When the edges have become firmer, take a small palette-knife and gently insert it between the clay and the edge of the paper "cast." Push the clay away from the sides of the paper, taking care not to split the papier-mâché, and gradually pull out chunks of clay. When you have removed all the clay, leave the paper halves to dry for 2–3 hours.

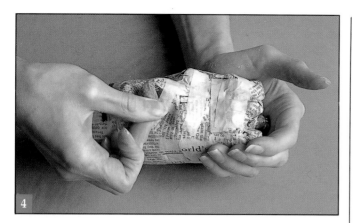

4 The two halves of the head now
need joining together again. Spread
a little undiluted white glue along
the edges of each half and fit them
together, holding them firmly in
place with masking tape. Make sure
that the edges fit neatly, or an ugly
join line will be visible. Let the glue
set for an hour, and then cover the
join with small strips of paper. Two
layers will be enough to seal it quite
tightly.

5 Now is the time to add more pronounced features to your puppet
with small amounts of paper pulp if
you want to. You will need long,
thin strips of paper. Dip them in the
wallpaper paste or watered-down
white glue, and scrunch them up
between your fingers, squeezing
out the excess glue. Arrange the
pulp directly on the puppet's head.
You can be quite flamboyant here,
and give your king a luxuriant
beard or your queen an ornate
crown. Let the pulp additions dry
for 24 hours. When they have dried,
cover them with a layer of small
paper strips and leave them to dry.

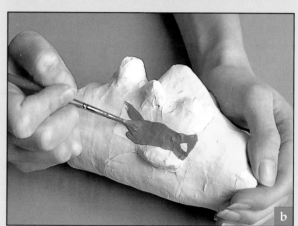

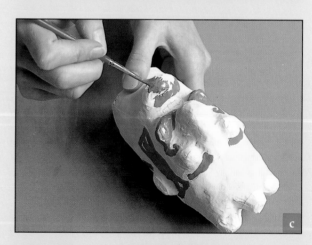

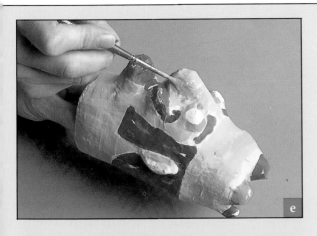

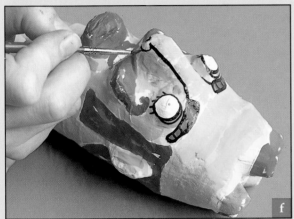

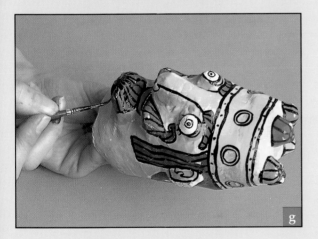

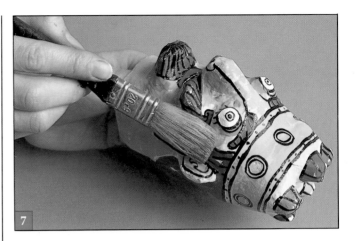

7 Leave the head to dry overnight and give it two coats of clear gloss varnish, allowing the first coat to dry thoroughly before you add the second. Clean your brush in soap and water when you have finished.

6 When the head is dry, sand it lightly and give it two coats of white paint. Draw in your puppet's features with pencil and start to fill them in with color. Leave the paint to dry for 4 hours, then define the face with black India ink.

Painting the puppet's head

Dressing your puppet

8 To make the clothes, trace the tunic patterns from the diagrams in the book onto tracing paper. Cut out the tracing-paper pattern and pin it to two thicknesses of felt. Cut carefully around the pattern and unpin it. Pin the two sides of the tunic together, right sides facing. If you have an adult to help you, the tunics can be sewn together by machine, or you can do it by hand. The seam should be about ¼ in. (5mm) from the edges of the material. Leave the neck open. Measure around your puppet's neck, and sew the neck opening of the tunic so that the head fits in snugly.

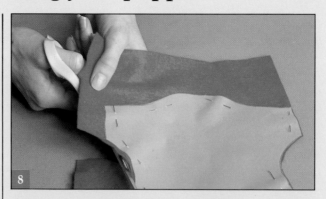

9 Trace the hand pattern from the diagrams onto tracing paper. Cut out the paper pattern and pin it to your felt. Cut out four hand shapes and sew two together for each hand, again leaving ¼ in. (5mm) for each seam. These seams will remain on the outside of the hands, so make your stitches as neat as you can. Cut lengths of gold braid to go around the sleeves and hem of the puppet's tunic. Sew the braid in place with running stitch.

10 Place one stitched hand just inside each sleeve. Pin through the sleeve to keep the hand in place and sew it to the sleeve with small running stitches. Stitch the excess sleeve material together and take out the pins.

11 Slip your puppet's head into its tunic to check that it fits. Smear a little strong, clear glue onto the puppet's neck and the inside neck openings of the tunic. Let the glue dry slightly, and then position the puppet's neck inside its tunic. Let the glue dry, and cover the join with gold braid. Stick this in place with strong, clear glue. Let your puppet dry overnight, and it will be ready to make its début!

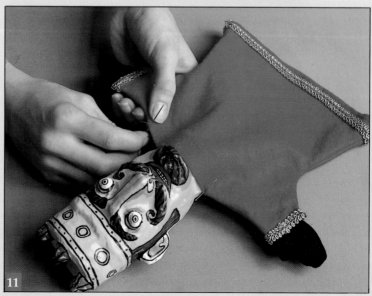

Unusual Papier-Mâché Objects

Mirror by **SANDY ENNIS** *of* **SURFACE SOLUTIONS**
Stained handmade paper on wooden support.

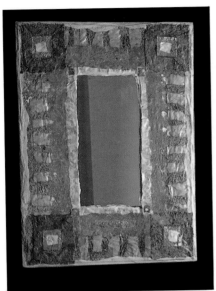

"Alpine Cow" by **FREDDIE ROBINS**

Papier-mâché on a styrofoam base.

Papier-mâché urn by **JACQUELINE SHELTON**

Hand built, stained with washes of color.

"Tattooed Ship's Cat" by **MARION ELLIOT**

Papier-mâché on styrofoam armature – decorated with gouache and black India ink and varnished with clear gloss varnish.

"James" by **SHEENA VALLELY**
AKA "Dirty Dog"

Papier-mâché on wire and newspaper armature, painted with acrylic paint.

"All the world's a stage," and everyone loves a puppet show.